WHEN GOD'S PEOPLE LET YOU DOWN

Books by Jeff VanVonderen

Families Where Grace Is in Place
Good News for the Chemically Dependent
The Subtle Power of Spiritual Abuse (with David Johnson)
Tired of Trying to Measure Up
When God's People Let You Down

WHEN GOD'S PEOPLE LET YOU DOWN

Jeff VanVonderen

BETHANY HOUSE PUBLISHERS
MINNEAPOLIS, MINNESOTA 55438

Published by Bethany House Publishers
A Ministry of Bethany Fellowship, Inc.
11300 Hampshire Avenue South
Minneapolis, Minnesota 55438

Printed in the United States of America.

Library of Congress Cataloging-in-Publication Data

VanVonderen, Jeffrey.
    When God's people let you down : how to rise above the hurts that
often occur within the Church / Jeff VanVonderen
        p.   cm.

    1. Church membership. 2. Christian life.
3. Church controversies. I. Title.
BV820.V26   1994
248.8'6—dc20   94-49032
ISBN 1–55661–348–2   CIP

Dedicated to those of God's family who, because of wounds and disappointments, are living more like strangers and exiles than precious sons and daughters. I'd like nothing better than to welcome you back home.

———

Special thanks to David Johnson, my fellow-laborer in grace. Before heaven, everyone should be able to have at least one friend like you.

JEFF VanVONDEREN, Director of Damascus, Inc., is an internationally known speaker and writer on addictions and church and family wellness. He served for twelve years as Counseling Pastor for Church of the Open Door in Minneapolis, Minnesota, and is currently the Teaching Pastor. He is also an instructor at Bethel College in St. Paul, Minnesota. Jeff is the co-founder and former director of Passages Counseling Center, a licensed Christian out-patient mental health clinic in Minneapolis. He is on the board of the National Association of Christian Recovery and a member of the American Association of Christian Counselors.

Jeff has a B.A. in Biblical Studies and Communication and a Master of Divinity degree. He has received advanced training from the University of Utah, University of Minnesota, and the National Institute on Drug Abuse in such areas as incest, domestic violence, assessment of mental health disorders, family systems, and the involvement of churches and schools in education/prevention of addiction. He has also received Minnesota Supreme Court certified training in mediation. He has authored several books and has also been published in various journals.

Contents

Part One

Introduction

You Want to Leave, but Something Won't Let You

Recently I heard a story about how part of the body of Christ went into action and regained ground lost to our secularized world. The story made me feel happy, even proud to be part of God's family. I tell it here because it contrasts so sharply with stories I hear from *inside* the family of God—true incidents of Christians deeply damaged by their brothers and sisters in Christ—some of them almost to the point of being driven away from God altogether.

I believe we have a problem in God's family, and only *we* can deal with it and heal the wounds of our brothers and sisters.

The story I heard on Christian talk-radio described a new Supreme Court decision that had threatened to set loose serious consequences for churches and other Christian groups. Texas school officials had refused to rent a building to a church group because they feared objections and lawsuits from the aggressive forces that hound conservative Christians. Though other community groups could rent the facility, Christians were denied access.

I'm always interested when I hear about the outside world pressing in on the family of God. Both as an individual Christian and the former co-pastor of a large Minneapolis church, I listened intently. Because of the urgent religious freedom issues involved, the church had decided to sue for the right to use the school building. The case worked its way up the judicial ladder all the way to the Supreme Court, which ruled that churches *must* have equal access to rental of public buildings, just like everyone else.

I smiled as I drove along, glad that God's family had won an important victory in the public arena. The radio host went on to point out that during the long legal battle Christians demonstrated remarkable unity. In petition drives. Phone calls to Congress. Prayer. Christians normally divided over doctrine and other issues pulled together. Once united, the family of God drove the secular wolf away from our door.

But as I switched off the radio and finished my drive home, another thought fought for my attention. We seem to be gaining skill at standing our ground and fending off the devastation that comes from those openly against the gospel. But in sixteen years of pastoring, counseling, and teaching in local churches—in Minneapolis, across America, and internationally too—I have met scores of dedicated, loving Christians who have been wounded-in-action. And they weren't hurt by "the liberal lobby" or by "unbelievers," but by brothers and sisters in Christ.

Wounds caused by people we count as friends are the most painful of all. The wounds we receive at the hands of other Christians—when not treated and healed—have devastating effects on us. And not only on us personally, but on how we relate to other Christians and even on how we relate to God.

Think about what happened when that one church in Texas felt the nipping "wolf" of secularism. What happened? Christians of all kinds heard the cry of others in the body, and from all across the nation believers poured out support, sweat, and prayer.

In fact, whenever an attack springs from outside the church, the effects look like this: Christians pray more, give more, serve more, trust God and trust each other more than ever before. In short, we *draw together*.

But when attacks and wounds come from *inside* the church, the exact opposite happens. We become wary, guarded, and grudging. We pray less, give less, serve less, and trust each other less. We sometimes even trust God less.

This is devastation at the deepest level, a wasting sickness of the soul and fiber of our own spiritual body.

How Can I Go On From Here?

We can't afford to have this damage continue unchecked and unhealed. Not only are the lives and hearts of individuals at stake, much bigger issues hang in the balance.

Several years ago, David Johnson and I wrote *The Subtle Power of Spiritual Abuse*, a book about the unwitting mistakes of otherwise well-meaning Christian leaders (including us). We identified how Scripture, authority, and spiritual gifts could be misused to control and manipulate people. We also wrote to expose leaders with dark intentions. We were overwhelmed by the volume of people who wrote to share their pain. Without a doubt, misused power in the church leaves a trail of wounded.

But misuse of authority by leaders is not the only way Christians get hurt in the church. We also hear from countless people who face neglect in times of great spiritual need. Or they feel persecuted because of giftedness. Or their openhearted giving is used and abused until they're used up—and then they're discarded. We heard from people stomped on again and again by brothers and sisters in Christ with unhealthy relationship skills whose destructive actions go unchecked by passive leaders.

The real surprise was this: After all the pain, most still asked, "How can I get involved in church again? I don't want to be hurt or used anymore, but I don't want to leave God either. And I want the fellowship with other Christians—but Christians who are *healthy.*"

Something inside these people continues to ask that question because the church, for all its weaknesses and failing, is a place of promise. They want to go to a new church, or go deeper in relationships in the church they are in. But they want to go in wiser, stronger, and healthier than before.

You Can Get There From Here

If what I have said describes your experience and your desire, then this book is for you.

You can get out of the hurt, frustration, and let-down feelings you are experiencing. I have to warn you that you will go down into the hurt itself before you climb up and out into the light. You clean a wound, not merely cover it over.

So in Part One of this book I will describe some of the ways we're let down by our spiritual families—and more than that, the inner damage that can go unchecked long after the event. We will learn what causes hurt so the next time we can step around the problem.

In Part Two, I will look at the enormity of grace, mercy, and health God wants to pour out to us through His family. So we'll be seeing what it means to be a member of God's family, to be His very own sons and daughters—with all the responsibilities and privileges that gives us as we relate to each other.

A Caution

To leaders who read this book: I have no interest in taking shots at the church from either a lofty perch of great understanding or from the sidelines. I write to confront the church about issues affecting the church from within the church—all in order that we may be healed together.

And I hope that if you feel hurt at the hands of the church you will not take up my words as a sword to stick those who stuck you. That won't help the healing of your heart or the body of Christ.

That isn't to say that I will never suggest confrontation. Person-to-person confrontation *is* sometimes necessary. Venting your anger may give you a moment of cathartic relief, but it isn't the true salve that will promote what you need once the offense is removed. In the end, only a mutual encounter with the Spirit of Truth can rebuild the relationships pain has destroyed.

So read before you react.

Ultimately, I want my writing and my life's work to do more than help individuals, important as that is to me. My purpose is to assist in the healing that's needed everywhere in the family of God. I hope that as you heal and grow stronger in spirit, this will become a purpose for your life too.

1

God Is Great, but I Don't Know About His Kids

I grieve when I think about Jerry. Out of commitment to Christ he served a nonprofit Christian organization faithfully for almost twenty-five years, for a salary so low that he and his family couldn't afford to buy a home or fund a retirement plan. But he accepted these limitations in order to do God's work.

Then the organization entered a couple of years of restructuring and upheaval. Internal politics began to make things rocky. In a crucial and tense meeting, Jerry was asked his opinion on a tricky issue on which various department heads held opposing vested interests. A man of integrity, Jerry offered his thoughts, knowing they ran counter to the opinion of the current leadership.

The next day, the head of the organization dismissed him. "We aren't sure we can count on your loyalty anymore, Jerry." Forget twenty-five years of evidence to the contrary. Jerry had the morning to clean out his desk.

Today, in his late fifties with no business training and without a strong resumé behind him, Jerry is stuck in a menial job. As far as involvement with Christians goes, he slips into church but won't stick around for "fellowship" afterward. He doesn't talk with anyone about God anymore.

On one hand Jerry sees his years of heartfelt faithfulness to God. On the other hand he sees how Christian brothers could not get beyond their own ego needs, how he was an organizational scapegoat. A dismal future in a low-income apartment is his thanks for a lifetime of service.

When Christians let us down, one of the biggest hurts is that we feel let down by God himself. After all, it was God's kid who sucker-punched us when we were open and vulnerable and unsuspecting, wasn't it? And where was *He* anyway? Why did He let us get hurt in the first place?

Wounds that happen to us within God's family have devastating consequences. You may realize that already. What you might not know is why it's so important to reopen painful experiences and take a deeper look inside. Here's why: The wounds we receive at the hands of other Christians leave us with unhealed gashes in our ability to relate to people. Not only that, they leave us with gaping holes in our relationship with God.

A Hard Look at the Damage

Let's be frank. For some people, the ruin and disappointment of a bad experience with other Christians is so painful that they exit the church for good. Considering the horror stories that come from within the body of Christ, it's understandable why some people aren't willing to try again. Many walk out the back door of the church and never go back—not to *any* church.

Others stick with the church to try to resolve relationship problems. But many of these people hit a frustrating wall: The harder they work to fix difficult relationships, the worse the situation becomes. When you fail to work things out with the very people who are supposed to be models of good will, patience, and understanding, that's disappointing.

Still others pick up and go across town. They plan to settle in a different church where they hope to find the healthy spiritual relationships they're looking for. But for many there remains a nagging doubt: *Will these relationships hold? Or will they fall apart again?* They wonder if they'll ever feel at home and relaxed with other Christians again.

I have found some common traits among folks who have been seriously damaged by brothers and sisters in the family of God. Let's look at a few.

The *first* common trait is that most Christians who are carrying wounds sense that they are in a bind. They aren't closed people by nature. They don't by habit shut people out. In fact, they *want* to believe they can be a healthy, contributing member of a church again. They want close friends again. But whenever they feel drawn to a church or to a spiritual friendship, inside them a red warning light flashes. It tells them, *Don't get close. It could happen again.*

If you have been deeply hurt by other Christians, I suspect you recognize in yourself the sense of wariness I'm talking about. It often causes the *second* trait I have noticed in wounded people. They keep a careful emotional distance.

They may be physically present at church, parked in the pew or on a folding chair. Yes, they enjoy singing and worship—anything that doesn't involve too much interpersonal interaction. Handshakes are still okay. Maybe a hug now and again. But beyond that they remain aloof in relating in a way that might require them to open up.

This contributes to a *third* trait. Some not only remain aloof, they've learned how to beat a hasty retreat. When pressure or confrontation is imminent, or when they're asked to make a commitment to something, they run. Sure, it was okay for them to retreat from the hurt caused in the past relationship—especially if they were emotionally and spiritually violated. Especially if they lacked leverage to stop the violations from happening over and over again. In that case, withdrawing was the safest thing to do.

But withdrawing leads these folks into something they hadn't bargained for, and that's a growing sense of isolation.

A *fourth* trait wounded Christians often experience is that they actually feel physical weariness at the thought of getting involved with church or other Christians again.

Every Sunday school teacher or pastor who was never allowed to take a real break from duty knows what I mean. A grave weariness often settles on Christians who have had to prove their commitment—to the church or to God—by the number of tasks they performed. Some felt pressure to shoulder too much responsibility. Some had to show their allegiance by scampering to church every time the doors opened. Some had to prove they were "in submission to authority" to satisfy the ego demands of a leader who didn't have the calling or the skills of a true spiritual shepherd.*

---

*To understand the forces at work in an abusive church you may wish to read *Tired of Trying to Measure Up* by Jeff VanVonderen, and *The Subtle Power of Spiritual Abuse* by Jeff VanVonderen and David Johnson, Bethany House Publishers.

A *fifth* trait is wandering from flock to flock. I have known lots of people blown from church to church, never able to sink roots, grow and bloom anywhere. They want to settle in, and they're even aware that they feel double-minded about church. Yet they can't escape this restlessness that makes them eye the door and wonder if something better lies in the next church down the block. . . .

Anything sound familiar?

The saddest part for me as a pastor is this: Before any of these folks understood what was happening, the family and friendships that are ours as children of God had dealt them some of the harshest disappointments and stinging wounds that any person can experience.

Perhaps you still attend church regularly. Maybe you even serve in some capacity. Or perhaps you stay on the fringes, like Jerry. The truth is that no matter what your actions look like on the outside, you cannot afford to ignore the leftover damage you carry inside. Not if you want to escape the bind of lingering negative emotions and the trap of isolation. Not if you want to move on to find healthy, growing relationships with other Christians. And with God.

Some hurting Christians spend the rest of their lives using non-involvement as a protective wall. That may seem to solve the problem. But on the down side, an uncomfortable feeling gnaws at them—and a dismal voice inside tells them, *You just don't fit in anywhere.* Or, *Don't let your guard down.* Or, *Nobody really knows about your needs—or cares.*

This is the voice of discouragement. And listening to it every day wears you down from within, I guarantee, unless you decide to take steps to silence it.

Our Wounded Are Everywhere, and They Need Our Help

What is going on in the body of Christ cannot be brushed off. If you have been wounded you know that's true. You may *try* to ignore the discouragement, the urge to protect yourself, and the distress of being let down. But it won't disappear just because you ignore it. It's unfortunate that the only advice you're likely to get from Christians is "C'mon, forgive and forget. Why can't you just let it go?"

The truth is that the wound you've received won't simply go away on its own. It's as if something has bitten you. Even if the exterior puncture heals, what's left is damage far beneath the sur-face. It's a deep-level wounding that will continue to victimize you and hurt your spiritual relationships.

I say this well aware of the backlash against "the victim men-tality" that has seized our culture. And rightly so. Doling out sym-pathy pats and allowing people to wallow in self-pity without of-fering real help and strength—this is worse than no help at all. Even so, I believe that victims need to be *shown* how to heal and become victors. Telling a person to pay no attention to their pain and fear won't help it go away. It just pushes it deeper where it can do even more damage.

If you've been wounded by God's people, I want to help you identify the mind-set that would leave you stuck in the mode of a perennial victim, always feeling sensitive and self-protective. We'll look at what makes for healthy relationships and interactions in the family of God. We'll explore the path that leads you through hurt and beyond into a new life of inner strength and fulfilling ser-vice to God.

But besides that, there are other important reasons why Chris-tians can't *afford* to ignore our wounded. No sane army com-mander looks out across a battlefield, sees his men shot and dying in dirt and blood but says to the medics, "Forget these guys. There's more where they came from." Too many Christians feel like good soldiers wounded in action—and the leaders and fellow soldiers who were supposed to notice and help have ignored them. What an added insult! You find yourself blamed for getting hurt in the first place.

Sad Faces in the Family Album

Before we go further I have to say that stories of hurting Chris-tians make me incredibly sad. Here are the experiences of several Christians whose faces are sad portraits in our spiritual family al-bum. Maybe you can find a likeness to your story in one of theirs.

———

Karen is a young mother who began to experience sudden panic attacks. Within weeks she was living under a cloud of dread and anxiety, constantly nagged by the feeling that something bad was about to happen, and that there was nothing she could do to stop it. She called friends in her church to pray for her. Then she went to her pastor for counseling, for any kind of help that would keep her from emotional disintegration. He was convinced she was hiding unconfessed sin and that her problems were the product of a guilty conscience. "Your problem is that you're in rebellion against God," he eventually told her.

The panic attacks became paralyzing, and then one Sunday morning, a month into her difficulties, she was horrified to hear herself used as a negative example in her pastor's sermon. Not by name, but that hardly mattered. Through the church's prayer chain everyone knew who he meant by "the young woman whose sin is causing her to suffer from terrible anxiety."

It's important to note that Karen eventually visited a doctor who discovered that she has a physical condition that caused her anxiety. A simple medication has eased her emotional suffering. But even though she attends a new church, the wound to her spirit remains. On one hand she remembers how vulnerable she was in the midst of her need, and on the other hand she sees how her confidence was betrayed and how she was judged for a hidden sin that didn't exist.

Then there's *Bill*. He was brought in to pastor a small struggling church—which responded with a spurt of growth to his caring heart, balanced knowledge of Scripture, and powerful sermons. Within a couple of years the congregation had raised enough money for the major building addition they needed for their building. These people insisted they wanted "strong Bible teaching." Bill was given authority to make several important decisions—but several elders and deacons didn't *like* his decisions.

They never discussed their feelings with Bill, however. Instead, their wives began a whisper campaign. The rumor mill churned out bigger and bigger stories, and eventually Bill was stunned when some unbelievable accusations were laid on him. The damage to the church was terrible, and Bill's reputation—not to mention his nerves and his will to go on—suffered immensely.

Bill nearly left the ministry. The dust cleared a little when the accusing faction left, but by then Bill had an angry and divided congregation on his hands. Now, when Bill thinks about the family of God he's been called to pastor, on one hand he sees his call to servant leadership and the climate of spiritual unity he works hard to build. And on the other hand he sees his congregation's lack of loyalty, coupled with the fact that Christians without a second thought could intentionally set out to destroy both his life's work and his good reputation. He's left with the sad weight of seeing what Christians are capable of doing to each other plus the insecurity of wondering if it could happen again.

————

Bob and *Lyn* left a conservative church to join a church where they heard from friends that "the Holy Spirit is really moving." They faithfully attended every special teaching seminar. They allowed themselves to have hands laid on them—and to fall over backward, "slain in the Spirit," mainly because everyone around them was falling down and they didn't want to be the only ones left standing up, looking as if they had "resisted" the Holy Spirit. Then they noticed how often various people came to them with directive "words from the Lord"—messages about Bob's business, or their marriage. Bob even sold some income property and gave the money to the church because he was told, "Thus says the Lord. *Sell.*"

Eventually, Bob woke up. If they listened to these "words," they would be turning over the decision-making responsibility for their lives to a group-think mentality. For one thing, none of these so-called "messages from the Lord" had any supernatural quality to them. They all concerned things commonly known about Bob and Lyn. And if they resisted or questioned anything, they were labeled "too independent" or "not in submission." When they decided to leave that church—not *the church*, but that particular congregation—they were warned that they were "rejecting the Holy Spirit."

Today Bob and Lyn on one hand look back at their open search for a closer, more dynamic relationship with God. And on the other hand they see how misguided Christians inserted themselves into that holy place of spiritual communion and direction that belongs only to the Lord.

————

On the outside *Al* is an ordinary-looking guy. But on the inside he's an extraordinary guy, gifted and intelligent. For years, he was the one who was there when anyone in his suburban church had a real need. Whether people needed prayer, spiritual encouragement, or help with everyday needs, his pastor counted on Al to share the load because Al was a model of love, servanthood, and practical insight.

When the church began to grow and needed new elders, two new guys in the congregation were appointed, while Al was overlooked. "I would have recommended you," the pastor told him, "but these guys are successful businessmen who know how to handle finances. I need leaders like them right now because we're going into a building-fund drive. Don't worry. We'll make you a deacon. . . ."

On one hand, Al hears his pastor preaching high ideals about spiritual qualities like service and Christlikeness. And on the other hand he sees the bottom line—how successful yet immature white-collar executives are placed in leadership positions when the Bible reserves those positions for men who demonstrate Christlikeness.

A House Divided

Each of these stories describes jagged cuts left in the hearts of faithful people—and not just the injuries they suffered personally, but the gaping wounds left unhealed within God's household, a wound full of pain, disappointment, doubts, and unresolved questions. (We'll deal more with the painful nature of this gap in Chapter two.)

Does the gaping space inside these people in any way resemble the torn feeling you have inside?

We know that unintentional hurts happen in every human relationship. That's life. We all know it.

But why would one Christian *intentionally* wrong another? And why is it that a Christian who *knows* he has wronged another compound the problem by refusing to acknowledge his wrongdoing? Why do we blame the victim? Why do Christians sometimes project *image, ego*, and *position* rather than respond in Christlike love to right their wrongs?

What's really going on when our relationships within the body of Christ suffer and we are ripped apart?

I believe that some big issues are at stake. What happens to us *personally* is important to God because He cares for each one of us. But when we became part of God's family, we also stepped into a *corporate identity*. In God's eyes, you and I are no longer just John or Jane Q. Individual. We have become so identified with Jesus and His brothers and sisters that Paul calls us members of the body of

Christ. This is hard for Christians today to grasp, considering the fact that we breathe ethers of *self-fulfillment, individuality,* and *independence* every minute of every day. But as Paul says,

> Now you are the body of Christ, and each one of you is a part of it (1 Corinthians 12:27, NIV).

And he also reminds us that God is the one who put us together as members of His body so that

> ... there should be no division (v. 25).

A sidenote: It's interesting that when Christians do terrible things or inflict injury on other Christians, nonbelievers immediately perceive the wrong. They're appalled. Yet they also seem to notice when Christians take responsibility for policing themselves and handling their own issues. They take note when Christians *act* like Christians. If *they* know when we're acting Christianly and when we are not—why do we muddle up right and wrong?

What I'm leading to is this: God had a plan in mind when He sent His Son, Jesus, into the world. I'm not referring to Jesus' death on the cross for our sins. I'm talking about another purpose. God sent Jesus to make us a people belonging to Him and supportive of each other. He sent Jesus so you and I and all other believers could be part of the "body of Christ," of which we have become members.

Unfortunately, God isn't the only one with a plan. Satan, who is God's adversary and ours, has a purpose too. We need to understand both God's purpose for His body and how our adversary works to destroy God's plans. Once we see the bigger picture, we can understand why Christians hurting each other is a life—and death—issue.

What the "Wolf's Bite" Is All About

As I said from the outset, the goal of this book runs deeper than helping you work through the hurts you have endured, important as that is to me. My goal—and someday *your* goal, as strange as it may sound now—is to bring health to the family of God. A lot depends on how you walk through the wounds you've received. A lot depends on the salve you apply to your pain. Let's take a look at the larger picture.

Jesus became man not only to save us from our sins but to restore us to a full, living relationship with the Father—the only true source of our life. That was His mission *on* the cross and *beyond* the cross.

And from the outset, the Adversary plotted to destroy Jesus and wreck His mission. Because Satan's intent was and always is to draw us away from God and into a dark eternity with him. So the struggle begins.

In Matthew 3 and 4, we see God give Jesus a fatherly pat on the back, saying, "This is my beloved Son, in whom I am well pleased." Immediately Satan moved in. We watch as Satan tempts Jesus to pull away from God and to seek life, honor, and security in created things—the exact temptations that are thrown at us. But Jesus stayed on course.

Satan did too. He had everything to gain by getting Jesus to turn away from the Father. So he mustered every force that would cooperate—from a swirling eddy of dark principalities in the heavenlies, to the earthly religious power brokers, to the brute strength of the Roman empire. If Jesus would not bow to Satan, He would have to be eliminated.

In some measure, the plan worked. Judas had been present to see the miraculous feeding of the thousands, and he had dipped his hand in the same dish as Jesus at the Last Supper. I don't want to trivialize the betrayal of our God by making a pun, but Judas really did bite the hand that fed him. And the rest of Jesus' closest friends let Him down by deserting and denying Him in His hour of greatest need. Is it possible that Satan was attacking Jesus with the same weapon he now uses on us—the bite of discouragement? Or the hurt of broken friendships that tempts us to give up on God?

Satan thought he had won. There hung Jesus, brutalized and nailed to a cross. And there He died.

Satan had accomplished his mission.

But so had Jesus.

Imagine the chaos in hell on the day of resurrection! (You might want to look at Ephesians 4:8–10 and 1 Peter 3:19). The huge barred door lay off to one side, bent and twisted from the entrance of God's Son over the weekend. In the ceiling there was a gaping hole, which He had blown open to make His exit. Cells were smashed. Manacles hung broken and useless. The evidence was everywhere: Satan would never have the total dominium and limitless number of prisoners he'd hoped for.

You can almost imagine Satan shaking his head in dismay, saying, "I should never have carried out that last mission." Now he finally understood that all along the Lord had had some higher plan—a purpose that made every dark thing regret that the Lord of Life had ever been murdered.

I've dramatized the story in this way so we can look at God's greater purposes in a new way. It's the larger picture Paul had in mind, I believe, when he wrote:

> . . . we speak God's wisdom in a mystery, the hidden wisdom, which God predestined before the ages to our glory; the wisdom which none of the rulers of this age had understood; for if they had understood it, they would have not crucified the Lord of glory (1 Corinthians 2:7–8).

What purpose and plan had God accomplished through the death and resurrection of Jesus? Winning our freedom from hell would have been enough to make the Adversary regret his assassination plot. But in fact there was much more.

Just before Jesus was betrayed, He revealed God's "hidden wisdom"—His "hidden plan"—to His disciples. He wanted to encourage them by letting them know what lay *beyond* His death. He told them,

> Truly, truly, I say to you, unless a grain of wheat falls into the earth and dies, it remains by itself alone; but if it dies, it bears much fruit (John 12:24).
> But the Helper, the Holy Spirit, whom the Father will send in My name, He will teach you all things, and bring to your remembrance all that I said to you . . . if I go, I will send Him to you . . . But when He, the Spirit of truth, comes, He will guide you into all the truth . . . (John 14:26; 16:7, 13).

Do you see Satan's real frustration? Because of Jesus' death, God's "hidden plan" is activated. Like seeds exploding from a ruptured seed-pod, a new kind of life—Life that generates life—spread as far as the wind can blow. *Satan didn't crush Jesus at all. He spread Him around!* After Satan killed Christ's body, the Holy Spirit not only resurrected Christ but birthed the body of Christ. No wonder God had concealed from the spiritual powers the mystery of the body of Christ.

And now what is clear is God's purpose for us, and Satan's hatred for us—a hatred so strong he would do anything to bite and devour us. Satan lost in his frontal attack—*the crucifixion* of Jesus. Now he would step up his guerilla attacks—the *infiltration* of Christ's body.

Christ Is Known Through the Church

Paul tells us that God has given us the Holy Spirit to bring us together into one body.

> ... in order that the manifold wisdom of God might now be made known through the church to the rulers and the authorities in the heavenly places (Ephesians 3:10).

This "manifold"—or "multifaceted"—wisdom of God included the plan to invade the world with light. The Lord of love came to light the darkness with the fire of the same kind of love He has for us. He created this body of believers so that we could befriend one another and struggle to stay faithful together—encouraging, comforting, and loving each other. He created this body so that we could live life with fullness, and that any in need would have their needs met (see 1 Corinthians 12).

The "rulers of this age" didn't have a clue of all that God was up to. Unfortunately, believers throughout time have also forgotten God's purpose for His body. From the Corinthians down through time to us, we have not grasped what made Satan shudder and angels shout: a vision of the Spirit-empowered body of Christ moving as one in love. Paul was careful to state his concern for the individual fights and factions happening in the Corinthian church in light of this greater concern.

Paul's concern needs to be our concern too, and it comes down to this: When the church does what God created it to do—when we demonstrate through our love and unity the glory of God's love—God mobilizes and strengthens us to change the world.

Is it any wonder that Satan, the Devourer, wants to tear Christ's body apart limb from limb?

The Wolf and You

We, the church, are God's proof to all powers in heaven and on earth that He has begun to reclaim the universe and reverse the Fall. And since Satan failed to stop Jesus, he turns his efforts to thwart God's working in and through the body of Christ. Since he can't defeat the Head of the family, he needs to destroy the children of the family. After all, he must have heard Jesus' promise to us (and a threat to him) when He said to the disciples, ". . . he who believes in Me, the works that I do shall he do also; and greater works than these shall he do" (John 14:12).

Greater works than these—can you see Satan's huge mistake? He let Christ conquer the crucifixion. Now Satan must do anything to stop God's powerful work-in-progress in the church.

Those "greater works" are we, the people of God, becoming the living embodiment of God's character and nature, accepted through God's new covenant and empowered by the Holy Spirit to spread goodwill to all. (In the next chapter, we'll take a closer look at what this "spiritual family heritage" involves.)

It makes sense that Satan's best offense now is to invade God's own family. If he can separate us from our brothers and sisters in Christ—whether in actual distance, or in our wounded hearts—well, maybe it is possible to blunt the conquering advance of God's Spirit after all!

In Acts, Paul warned the elders in Ephesus to "be on guard for yourselves and for all the flock . . . savage wolves will come in among you, not sparing the flock" (Acts 20.28, 29). No doubt this referred to attacks from without, specifically men who wanted to pull believers back into the legal bondage of Judaism. But he also warned that "from among your own selves men will arise" (v. 30), predicting that attacks on individuals in the body would come from the most dangerous, least suspect place of all—from *within* the church.

The apostle James makes clear that the destruction of the church really is the work of Satan when he wrote:

> If you have bitter jealousy and selfish ambition in your heart . . . this . . . is not that which comes down from above, but is earthly, natural, demonic (James 3:14, 15).

In fact, most of the book of James (Chapters 2 through 4) describes various things that wound Christians and cause disunity in the body: favoritism, distinctions, quarrels and conflicts, speaking against one another, and judging.

Now be clear about something. I am *not* saying that the Christian who hurt, disappointed, or betrayed you is "*the* Wolf," or even "*a* wolf." Because a brother or sister lets you down—even intentionally—doesn't mean he or she is demonic, the embodiment of evil. So take this warning: Please do not use this book as an excuse to launch a demon hunt or to demolish another Christian with a volley of bitter judgments—because you would only be participating in the tearing down that the apostles warn us about!

David Johnson and I noted in *The Subtle Power of Spiritual Abuse* that sometimes it's necessary to separate yourself from a particular church or other Christian groups in order to spare yourself further abuse and to wrestle free to grow in the grace of Christ. But there is another alternative. Assuming that the atmosphere in your church or other Christian relationships allows for healthy change, you *can* help bring good out of painful situations.

Unfortunately, those words are probably being read by the Christians who *get* ulcers, not those who *give* them. Some circumstances won't change. The people causing the problem may refuse to change. But you and I can't afford to sit by, wishing that other people would make the church what it should be—what God intends it to be because of our involvement. When nothing changes and we continue to complain and withdraw—if not our physical presence, then our inner commitment—we lose and so does the body of Christ.

Beyond Hurt to Health

Working through your pain and embarking on God's mission to bring healing to the church is easier said than done, isn't it? Finding your way feels impossible. Yet there are steps that can help you find once again a healthy interaction with the church. In fact, the tug we feel pulling us back to this spiritual family is a mark that the Holy Spirit is still active in us. That He wants to lead us to true healing. And that He cares too much to let us go away easily!

In the chapters that follow we will walk through steps that lead to healthy Christian relationships that give us personal fulfillment through the rightful support and encouragement we need to eventually retake our place of service in God's family.

When push comes to shove and we feel driven from the body, you and I can't afford to let the fact that other Christians have let us down keep us from taking part in the life-giving purposes of our God. It's an issue not just of wanting to thrive, but to survive. Our own health and growth are at stake—and so is the work and witness of the church as it offers the world light and hope. It's possible that the pain and anguish you have faced, once healed, will be transformed into the wisdom and compassion you need to help another Christian struggle to freedom, wholeness, and peace.

For now, though, feel free to rest, to let God mend your soul before you hurry about fixing others' broken hearts. Use this book as a tool for healing. God wants to heal the "Wolf bite" that's causing you anguish. Your own well-being and the well-being of other Christians will benefit from the time you take now to meet our healing, loving God—possibly at deeper levels than ever before.

2

A Welcome Place in God's Own Family

"I can't believe we were ripped off by *Christians!*" says Gary. A Christian ministry hired his consulting company to develop a major project. But after Gary's company completed the work, the ministry's president told Gary they couldn't pay.

"He told me their contributions took a nose dive this year—but he has faith they'll be able to pay me *eventually*. He said, 'We're praying about our financial needs every day—and we're praying that you'll be blessed, brother.' These people told me when they signed the contract that they had money set aside for this project in a special account. Now I find out they really didn't have the money. I've had to lay off one of my support staff, and creditors are barking at me. These ministry people didn't have *faith*—they had presumption. They lied."

Gary's summary of the situation is the saddest part: "How can Christians use *Christianity* and *faith* and all this *brother* stuff to take advantage of another Christian? I'd like to say I trust my brothers in Christ—but this isn't the first time Christians have come to me with a 'give-me-something-for-nothing' attitude. I'll think twice before I'm that trusting with other Christians again. And, in fact, the next time someone calls me 'brother' I'll double the price."

———

In the first chapter we looked at stories of Christians whose bad experiences with other Christians marked them deeply. The stories are real, though names and details have been changed to protect privacy. Yet I can say that none of these folks are "negative" or "crabby" or "cynical" or even "unwilling to forgive." Every one of them wants to forgive and go on. But like Gary, each one is left with a terribly uneasy feeling inside—what we referred to as a "big gap."

I don't think that those I've described are critical people out to find fault. What I do think is that many good Christians suffer insult on top of injury after they've been wronged. How? By being told they should gloss over what happened and deny that they feel let down, or to act out forgiveness they don't have—to "fake it till they feel it." Sadly, the whole body of Christ suffers. Why? Because when we don't take the appropriate steps to handle wounds between Christians, individual Christian relationships and even whole churches become full of fake forgiveness. Our goal is to grow into healthy relationships. And in any human relationship there will be hurt—for iron to sharpen iron you need a whole lot of friction. But stresses and character weaknesses *have to be* worked out before strong, true bonds are formed.

We can't dismiss the body's hurts any longer. So as a first step toward healing it's important to look at why wounded Christians are often misunderstood, blamed, and wounded further. We will also look at what happens when our ability to relate on a deep trust level with other Christians is damaged and left unhealed.

What Did You Expect?

Occasionally I hear a pastor or a Christian counselor comment about hurting Christians who come to them for help. Most are sympathetic and want to encourage healing. But sometimes I hear statements like this:

> Their whole problem is that their expectations were too high.
> They need to know that other Christians aren't perfect, just like they themselves aren't perfect.

They may even toss in that famous bit of bumper-sticker wisdom: "After all, Christians aren't perfect, they're just forgiven." Even worse, I think, is the thinking that gives us these gems:

> They had a negative expectation, so they *got* a negative experience.
> They had a negative confession—and confessed they were hurt—so that's why negative things happened to them.

That line of thinking has more to do with the cultic metaphysical reasoning of Christian Science than with biblical Christianity.

Yes, it's true that some of us in the church are oversensitive souls. We all know people who take offense at everything, who notice every wrong note played by the pianist and every misquote of Scripture by the pastor. But certainly not every Christian who's been wronged fits into that category. We can't write off legitimate concerns. We can't deny real problems.

I want to emphasize an important point for leaders in the body of Christ. But don't skip over the next couple of paragraphs if you're a person-in-the-pew Christian, because every one of us needs to learn how to lead in the areas of our own lives by growing in personal living skills.

Often I find that leaders lack relationship skills. I'm painting myself into the picture when I say this. Trust me—my work has pried open my eyes to my own needs in this area!

What I have observed is that leaders often can't relax and be *themselves.* They erect a self-sufficient shell and let no one see their failings or inadequacies. They don't form open, vulnerable friendships. The result? They build organizations and churches that are weak in healthy relationships. On the other hand I've observed that the strongest, most dynamic spiritual leaders are those who acknowledge their weaknesses and are willing to *demonstrate* growth—as opposed to preaching about it, or demanding from their flock what they themselves have not learned how to do. After all, people follow leaders who lead by example.

What I'm saying is that every one of us as Christians—leaders included, leaders *especially*—plays a part in building stronger Christian relationships and also in building healthy local Christian bodies. And the family of God can't afford for any one of us to dismiss another Christian's wounds or to bandage hurts with glib words that have no more depth or compassion than bumper-sticker slogans. As a Christian who has willingly accepted a leadership role, I remind myself daily that the people watching me will learn how to relate better to each other as I learn, practice, and demonstrate good relationship skills. And the points where I refuse to grow are where they likely will get stuck as well.

Back to expectations. I believe it helps to begin with the realist's perspective: Every one of us *has* expectations we bring when we come together with the family of God. Rather than write off someone's expectations as wrong, we should wonder *why* those expectations exist. Where did they come from? If we are honest we will admit that many of the expectations we consider too high are expectations that come from God: Love one another. Accept one another as God has accepted us. Encourage one another daily. Say nothing except what builds up.

When we dismiss a brother's or sister's expectations as excessive, we should first ask if we are allowing God to draw us into a family where we can love or be loved, or if we are backing off from God's plan for us.

I believe God created each of us with certain longings that can only be fulfilled in healthy physical families, and also some spiritual longings that in God's wisdom can only be fulfilled in a spiritual family. Not only did He create the longings, He also created the setting in which those longings could be fulfilled. And in the case of our spiritual needs and desires, the setting is the church—not the place with four walls, but in among the sheltering walls of God's living stones, His people.

Deep and Wide

Recently, a local television station broadcast a story that knotted my throat—a story that topped the evening news.

A small, anxious crowd filled a gate area at the Minneapolis airport. The anticipation was high as the reporter waited with a local family, plus their friends and relatives, for a special arrival from overseas. Drawn by the lights and camera crew no doubt, dozens of busy travelers stopped to see what the rising excitement was all about. The camera focused on the door of the tunnel-like ramp leading from the jetliner that had pulled up to the terminal. The eagerness on the faces of that waiting family was worth a million dollars.

As we all waited, the reporter filled us in.

The story had begun in the Philippines, where many children are abandoned to the streets. One small boy, only thirteen months old, had been abandoned and left to starve in a garbage-choked alley in Manila. That's where church workers found him. They took him to a Christian orphanage and named him Joe.

Enter a family from Minnesota who dreamed of opening their home and their hearts to this abandoned little boy. And now on my television screen I could see their faces as they waited.

The door opened and out stepped a woman—carrying in her

arms the cutest little guy. Baby Joe. The crowd burst into cheers, and the new parents rushed to take him in their arms. A banner they brought said it all. *Welcome to our family!*

The tears running down my face were accompanied by a goofy smile. *Good for you, Joe,* I thought. One small child, who could have perished in a stinking dark alley, had found a home and a family. He would live and grow up surrounded by love.

Now some of you may resist the sentiment this story raises. But unless we have stone-cold hearts, I think it speaks volumes to us.

Getting a new family is a big deal. So big it can make the evening news, so big that total strangers stop their busy lives to watch a childless couple embrace an abandoned child and make him their own. Can't you feel that? Don't you long for that? Why do people cheer and cry at the sight of a new family, whether in an airport gangway or hospital maternity wing? For the same reason, I think, that we go to movies about kids, dogs, cats, and animal babies lost in the wilderness, fighting their way home. Because inside we recognize that the longing and the struggle is *our* story too.

Why? Because we all tussle with life and its confusion and toughness. We hope to find a safe place to let down our struggle and simply *belong*. Just as we are. Without one plea. We long to find people who will take us into their lives—to care about us, to encourage us, to teach us, to lovingly help us see our weaknesses and constructively help us learn how to grow stronger. To just want our company.

At the risk of having you get stuck on the sentiment and not look past it to see the core of truth: When we become Christians we are all like baby Joe, coming out from the dark stink of this world, wanting to be taken into a spiritual home, a spiritual family where we're free to live, to make mistakes as we learn, and to grow stronger. Our desire is called *hope*—and it's the breath of life to our soul.

We may dismiss animal stories as fairy tales, but we can't forget or forsake the hope that springs from our souls.

When we come to church, when we get in among our new spiritual family, we *hope* we have found the place where we can safely rest and let down our guard. We hope we have found a place where life is lived differently than it's lived out in the world. Where self-centeredness is replaced by coming together around the higher purposes of God—by causes and goals and ideals that sweep us up in their bigness, where selfish ambition is replaced by preferring each other. Where greed is replaced by generosity—or, at the very least, freedom from worry that someone will manipulate money out of us for a cause that isn't what it appears to be.

So here we stand, all alone, knowing our deep needs. We see something that raises in us hope of fulfilling those needs. Even so, right before us lies a black chasm of anxiety and fear. What if our needs can never be fulfilled? What if we're stuck here alone forever, lonely and needy? There on the other side of the chasm is this shining group of people, the family of God. Everything inside us now shouts, "Let down your guard! Go over to them and open up! They can help you get your needs filled, your hopes met!" (Doesn't everything about these people exude promise? Including their Bible, and their advertisements for "fellowship"?)

So you decide to leave your self-protective stronghold, because the isolation is killing you. How do you get over to the other side, where the bright, happy-looking, promiseful people are? You lay down a thin, shaky little bridge of hope and scuttle over the dark chasm of dread. At last you're on the other side!

And now that you've made it to the other side and you stand amid God's people, what do you find?

Excuse Me, but I'm Confused

I don't believe many of us expect to find a church home where the kind of spiritual camaraderie I have described is in *perfect* working order. I have met far too many reasonable, realistic Christians to think that all our disappointments stem from unrealistic expectations. More often, I meet Christians whose hurt and disappointment come from something utterly reasonable. We joined ourselves to churches and to other Christians because we hoped they would operate with a different set of values than the world. We hoped they would value honesty over backbiting, fair-dealing over cheating, helping people to grow through weakness rather than condemnation or judgment.

Take Margie, for example: "I went to my pastor because I'd been feeling spiritually dry—kind of like flat soda pop." She says, "For one thing, I'd been teaching the same Sunday school class for *years* and I asked for a relief teacher. I felt drained. He told me that one of the parents had complained about me—but he wouldn't say who—and had asked him to replace me anyway. That was bad enough, but then came the real slap. He said that ever since I'd become a widow—my husband died two years ago—I'd become very negative. He told me, 'We just can't let your negative spirit affect the children anymore.'"

Was Gary unreasonable when he hoped that a Christian ministry would be honorable and not deceive him in doing business? Was Margie unreasonable to hope for support from her pastor—or wrong to feel let down when what she asked for was legitimate relief from both inner and outer burdens?

For many Christians, the root of the problem is that they have invested their trust in their brothers and sisters in Christ. They've invested money and hours of labor as well, only to have what they offered misused, thoughtlessly thrown in the mud. Their ability to *hope* has taken a severe blow, along with their will to invest themselves one more time when they already have given up so much. In short, they hoped that they wouldn't find the same spirit at work in God's family that is at work in the world. So was the problem that their expectations were too high?

No. Remember God's purpose for sending Jesus? It wasn't only to die for our sins, but to gather us into a family. And God has given us some clear marks of what His family will look like when He is the true Head. Those marks, which we will look at throughout this book, need to become our goals, personally and corporately. I don't believe we can allow the Wolf to degrade the people of God until they bear more resemblance to *him* than they do to Jesus Christ.

For now let's look at one of the most important, basic characteristics of a strong spiritual family. It's one of the big reasons we all have hopes and expectations of the body of Christ in the first place.

Welcome to the Family!

A healthy biological family provides a safe place where little humans can begin to learn about life and love and living. A human family—operating the way God made it to operate—offers safety, help, encouragement, allegiance, support, and understanding to all its members. It bestows these life-giving gifts free of charge—not because they are earned. (For a further look at this, see *Families Where Grace Is in Place*.) Likewise, the church—when it is a healthy spiritual family—offers these gifts free, also.

In fact, the family of God is meant to offer this kind of safe, grace-filled relationship to an even greater degree because it represents Jesus. And as Paul says,

> So then you are no longer strangers and aliens, but you are fellow citizens with the saints, *and are of God's household*; having been built upon the foundation of the apostles and prophets, Christ Jesus Himself being the corner stone (Ephesians 2:19, 20, italics added).

Hope draws us to Christ so we can find a solution not only for our sin problem but for our loneliness, grief, and confusion. Hope makes us look for a place where our soul can be "safe at home." What is the sign that hangs outside a spiritually safe place? Jesus told us when He prayed for all His disciples throughout time:

> . . . that they may be *perfected in unity*, that the world may know that Thou didst send Me (John 17:23, italics added).

Being "perfected in unity" means more than agreeing on doctrines. It also means a oneness in heart that comes when we know we can *trust* and *be trusted*. Real unity includes mutual respect, mutual support, mutual encouragement in growth, mutual tolerance and mutual help in weakness. Those things, I believe, are what Jesus meant when He asked God to help us progress in the process of being "perfected in unity."

Here's the catch: If our spiritual families and our "siblings" in Christ don't provide a setting ruled by safety in spirit and mutual trust, there's a big problem. We can't grow *personally* or in the *corporate oneness* Jesus prayed for. And if our unity has no depth beyond mental agreement to a list of doctrines, how can we expect anyone to believe Jesus is our Lord and Savior through and through?

More Serious Than You Thought

The family of God was created to be our place of spiritual safety, to provide relationships where we can open our hearts unafraid that we will be misused because we know that others are committed to our well-being.

God's design for His family is always balanced and healthy. Jesus doesn't intend to set you or any other Christian up to be abused by meeting someone else's self-centered, excessive needs.

To be sure, one day you may grow so strong in your knowledge and awareness of God's life within you that you choose to set aside your needs to help another who is in greater need. But that isn't the same as being used and used up by other Christians who confuse their whims—their selfish ego needs—with true, God-given spiritual needs. Helping others in the family of God doesn't mean swallowing the lie that it is God's will for you to be drained dry by meeting other Christians' self-protective, fear-inspired demands.

In the family of God we meet each other's needs by together drinking from the real Source of life. When a group of empty, needy people try to get their needs met by each other, all you'll find is a whole lot of consuming going on. Only as we learn to draw life from God—*the Source*—do we stop overdrawing from each other's inner *resource.*

You see, God's kingdom residents—His own family—are called to be a living, walking semblance of Jesus Christ, filled with life by the Holy Spirit dwelling in us and flowing from us. By "semblance of Jesus" I mean doing what He did; always pointing people to the Father, the Giver of inner life. The world offers its residents criticism and slavery. As residents of God's kingdom we are to offer each other acceptance and support.

Is it any wonder that the damage goes so deep when another Christian violates our trust at such a profound level? A relationship that you thought would give you hope and support and growth, instead pushed you down and took something away. Even worse, it opened the door to an evil whisper: "If this is how the people who represent Jesus act, then maybe He really isn't who He claims to be after all."

Is it any wonder that our Adversary, the "Wolf," majors in destroying relationships inside the body of Christ? Is it any wonder he wants to drive people out of the church altogether? In either case, his goal is to drive you back across the chasm of fear where you live isolated and alone in your self-protection. Completely on your own, without true spiritual brothers and sisters to warn you when he sneaks up on your blind side, you are much easier prey.

Now I'm aware that a couple of dangers crop up in talking about Satan at this point.

The first danger is the fact that the threat of Satan may already have been used to manipulate you. It happens in churches everywhere. You may have been told, in order to keep you in a destructive situation, that Satan lurks just outside the supernatural glow of a particular church or relationship. You may have heard the threat that you could find safety only if you stayed "under the covering"— *even though the church or individual made no attempt to change the things they did to contribute to the problem.*

That isn't what I'm talking about here. In fact, no one can find true spiritual strength or healing when they are stuck in that kind of manipulative situation. So if someone uses Satan's power as a threat to instill fear in you to manipulate you into staying in a spiritual trap, *get out now.*

How do you recognize this danger in a church or in a relationship? A trap is where the bait of hope is dangled before you—hope that hurtful or destructive things will get better and your real spiritual needs will get met—soon. In the meantime you feel yourself being hurt over and over again, and *the other side makes no real effort to change, only makes empty promises.*

That death-dealing situation only changes when one party does whatever it takes to get healthy.

There's a *second danger* involved in talking about Satan when there are hurts between Christians. You could, of course, make the mistake of thinking that every Christian who hurts or disappoints you is Satan's tool and begin to accuse your enemies of being satanic. Nonetheless, the real danger here—the diabolical element that tries to take over when you get wounded—is that you become fixated on the people or situations that hurt you. You could become one of those people who says, "Because I was hurt by Christians . . ." or "Because I was deceived by a Christian leader . . ." therefore, "I won't trust Christians ever again—and I'm definitely not committing myself to a church again!" And as long as you focus on the people or the hurtful situation, you won't see how you dangerously isolate yourself in your single-handed attempt to avoid further hurt.

Do you feel the inner isolation I'm talking about? Maybe you sense it so acutely that sometimes it's unbearable. To be on your own, caring for yourself, meeting your own needs—that is a lifestyle of isolation. You can become really good at living without the trusting, supportive relationships of others. But it's exactly the opposite of the blessing God had in mind for you when He called you into His family, a place of freedom to be you, where you can grow from weakness to strength.

The Spiritual Family Blessing

One of the main goals of this book is for you to regain the blessing of a strong spiritual family. It's what we need. It's what God has intended for us.

But it's a "catch-22," isn't it? You *want* safe spiritual relationships—but you fear trying again because you were fooled the first time. What looked safe *wasn't*. You feel knotted inside because you actually want something—true spiritual fellowship—but that's the very thing that booted you back over that dark chasm. With friends like that . . .

I want to set you free from the inside, so free that you are willing to try again. But what will keep you from being fooled again? Here's what will: the strength of a new understanding about the body of Christ and about yourself. And the strength of a better relationship with God that grows as you press through your disappointment to find Him again.

I need to tell you that there are no rock-solid guarantees. I can't assure you that no Christian will ever let you down again.

But what I can do is provide you with a greater understanding of what God intended the body of Christ to be. Unfortunately, we'll also have to look at the negative side — what God did *not* want His family to be. But armed with the positive picture, you can begin to move into Christian relationships again with confidence. Like a buyer of gold or jewels, once you know the *genuine article*, you can spot fakes right away.

Before we look at the first characteristic of healthy Christian relationships, I want to close this chapter by encouraging you to do two things:

First, accept no substitutes when it comes to finding a spiritual family and healthy relationships.

Second, don't stop looking until you've found them.

I can assure you that other hopeful Christians are out looking just as hard as you are. And greater health will come to you *and* the body of Christ as soon as you find one another.

3

What Is a Healthy Spiritual Family?

Marie was a nineteen-year-old woman who had made an appointment to see me for counseling, saying she needed to talk about "depression and anxiety."

As she sat down opposite me in my office, I opened our first session by asking how I could help.

She hesitated, her face betraying great conflict. She looked down and coughed. She stared at her hands, which were busily wringing a tissue to shreds in her lap. I waited for her to begin describing the emotional turmoil that was so obvious. Instead, after a long pause, she looked up. The desperation in her eyes was terrible as she asked, "Are you a mandatory reporter?"

With her question the reason for Marie's painful conflict came clear. In Minnesota, as in some other states, the law requires professional caregivers to report cases of abuse and neglect, so that authorities can advocate for those too weak to advocate for themselves. It is illegal for a professional caregiver *not* to report even suspected abuse.

So Marie had revealed her problem without having said a thing about it. I recognized her manner as the wary approach of someone carrying long-buried fear. Inwardly, she stood on the far side of the chasm fear had trenched, looking over at me. For her to cross over to safety she again had to place her hope in the very thing that had already caused her so much pain. She had to decide whether she could open up again and trust someone who represented *authority*.

I had to state the fact, of course, that I am obligated to report abuse. But now that she knew that fact, would I ever be able to create an atmosphere where she felt free to share her story—when she obviously knew that doing so was going to upset a big apple-cart in somebody's life? Her own included? Or when she knew that revealing the problem would bring her pain before relief?

And beyond the facts, beyond upsetting reality, I detected another question in Marie's eyes. The answer to her unspoken question would cost me something *and* cost her something. To build a trusting relationship requires both parties to make an investment: Trust must be met with trustworthiness. Underneath it all, the emotional root of her question was this: *Am I safe with you? Or are you going to abuse me too? Or are you just going to report this and not really care about what happens to me?*

I understood her hesitation. It came from wariness, and now I saw it in her eyes—actually in her whole demeanor. She displayed the inward turning of someone who has suffered in helpless, silent anguish far too long.

Marie did trust me with her story, and in a later chapter we'll look at the outcome. For now, I want to revisit two points we touched on in the opening chapters.

Trust and *spiritual safety* go hand in hand. When our trust is met with trustworthiness we feel safe. The more safe we feel, the more freely we open up and bring what is hidden away in the dark inside us out into the light. I believe that this is in part what John had in mind when he wrote:

> This is the message we have heard from him and declare to you: God is light; in him there is no darkness at all. . . . But if we walk in the light, as he is in the light, we have fellowship with one another, and the blood of Jesus, his Son, purifies us from all sin (1 John 1:5, 7, NIV).

How can we walk free from pain—and how can we step loose from our sin—unless we find the safe places to unpack our burdens? How can we become free to stop fighting the war to self-justify, self-protect, and self-exalt in an effort to look "good enough" in the eyes of others? Who will help us to see our way through our emotional bondage and our life-dominating habits that lead us again and again into sin? Who will help us to grow out of these things, I ask, if our spiritual family won't?

Where's All This Light Coming From?

Learning together to walk "in the light" builds an atmosphere in God's family in which emotionally healthy growth happens. And it builds the spiritual safety zones we need to clearly perceive the roots of our sin. But this deep-level trust building doesn't happen just by hanging out a sign and calling ourselves a church, a fellowship, a Bible study, a prayer group, or a support group. Calling yourself Mickey Mouse doesn't mean you'll grow big black ears, nor does calling yourself a follower of Jesus mean you'll be able to trot across the surface of the Sea of Galilee on your next sightseeing trip to Israel. We don't become spiritual safety zones by *calling* ourselves anything. We must *become* what we claim to be.

Churches frequently build what we call "fellowship" around just about everything besides true trust. We fellowship around doctrines we agree on—or just as often, we fellowship around an *interpretation* of doctrines that fit what we already believe. Or we fellowship around a pastor's showcased talents. Or around our belief in supernatural gifts, or the belief that today there are no supernatural gifts in operation. Or around the way we like our worship to look—or how well put-together the men look, or how women and children behave, or how families function. Or how we vote. We fellowship around food, and around special teaching series. We fellowship around "outreach" ventures to get people "saved."

But do we fellowship around "in-reach" ventures? Even in churches that are structured on cell groups, care groups, prayer and share groups—do we really know what spiritual support means?

All the things I've mentioned above are *types* of fellowship— but they involve fellowship around outward things. Each one has importance, in its place. But not one provides the level of trust building needed to promote spiritual growth, emotional stability, and healthy lives that overflow in freedom and happiness.

Who wouldn't be drawn to this kind of fellowship? What pastor wouldn't want to lead such a group? Wouldn't this breed of spiritual family be like "a city set on a hill," pulling people out of darkness to the glow of its light? (Matthew 5:13–16) Surely many would be attracted to our churches—and to us as God's representative people—if we began to live what Paul describes:

> Let no debt remain outstanding, except the continuing debt
> to love one another, for he who loves his fellow man has ful-

filled the law . . . *love is the fulfillment of the law* (Romans 13:8,
10, NIV, italics added).

The One Main Rule of God's Household

Human beings are incredibly needy. In nature, baby animals
mature and become self-sufficient at a fantastic rate. A newborn
deer is up and walking in hours. In weeks, baby birds are flying,
cracking open seeds, scratching to find bugs. We humans take forever just to learn how to be *physically* self-sufficient.

And besides our basic outer needs for food and shelter and the
like, we have basic inner needs too. We need to know that we are
loved, without strings—loved *regardless of behavior*. Love that you
have to work for doesn't build and refresh. It tears you down. Love
that has to be earned will eventually exhaust you.

Likewise, we need to know that we have *worth*, and that our life
has *purpose*. We also need to know that we are *not isolated* in our
problems, that other people struggle and fall, struggle and learn,
just as we do. And we need to know that others will *support* us
through our learning and failures as we make honest attempts
(and sometimes dishonest attempts) and *grow strong*. And we
need to be entrusted with the properly balanced weight of responsibilities in order to *mature* and not continue to live as a weak,
dependent person.

I have mentioned a few of the inner needs of every human
heart. Even if I perceive myself as on top of life—strong and successful—I kid myself if I think I have outgrown these needs. Our
need for *love, worth, purpose, support, growth* and the need to
carry the responsibilities of *maturity*—these are the things that
cause us to grow in greater health in our spirits.

Now a person who grew up without a family to count on can
tell you it's wonderful to go from having no one to count on but
yourself to belonging to a real live family—that is, if the adopting
family understands how to help meet these inner needs.

In the same way, it's an awe-striking thing when we become a
member of a spiritual family—so long as the spiritual family that
takes us in knows how to help meet our inner needs. (We'll look
more carefully at *how* spiritual needs are met as we go on.) In becoming a Christian, not only do we pass from spiritual death to life
but we cease being spiritual orphans. We become members of
God's family. This is how Peter describes it:

But you are a chosen race, a royal priesthood, a holy nation, a people for God's own possession, that you may proclaim the excellencies of Him who has called you out of darkness into His marvelous light; for you once were not a people, but now you are the people of God; you had not received mercy, but now you have received mercy (1 Peter 2:9–10).

Once, again, we come face-to-face with the human need to be let out of private spiritual darkness and into light. And this time, out in the light, we see the company we're among—a group of other lone, lost souls. And the relationship bond that ties us together is that we have "received mercy." As Peter says, *God himself* "called us out of darkness" *by* His mercy to *receive* His mercy.

Christians have been taught that we are saved by *grace*, unearned, undeserved favor. God gives us strength and power, benefits we didn't work for. He comes alongside of us to enable us to live life. He builds into us wellness and worth. But we rarely hear teaching about *mercy*. Mercy is the counterpart to grace—and by that I mean that mercy is unearned, undeserved forgiveness and love.

Both mercy and grace are spiritual treasures that become ours when God himself adopts us into His family. They are part of what Peter refers to as the Christian's "inheritance which is imperishable and undefiled and will not fade away" (1 Peter 1:4). A moment later Peter says that we have been born again "not of seed which is perishable but imperishable, that is, through the living and abiding word of God" (v. 23).

When we were born again, we obtained a spiritual inheritance—and that inheritance isn't like money guardedly stuffed away in a safe-deposit box. It's like a "seed" God planted in us so that a new, undying spiritual man or woman can be reborn and grow out of the old one, which is passing away. And so the inheritance we've received is this: *We have been given new genes.* The genes we inherited when we were adopted into God's family are pretty incredible.

And one of the most powerful and life-giving seeds God planted in you and in me is the seed of mercy—a love and forgiveness we can offer to each other that is free, unearned, just as God's mercies for us are "new every morning" (Lamentations 3:23).

Here's the point: In our relationships within God's family—as in our personal relationship with God—the number one rule is "Love one another." And as the saying goes, rule number two is

"When in doubt, refer to rule number one."

Earlier we saw that when we became Christians we took on a corporate identity. Now we have to face another fact: When we became part of the body of Christ we entered into a new kind of "family government," so to speak. And the rule of the household is love.

Hold On a Minute

"It's fine to talk about love," you may be thinking. "Love is a great ideal. But I've never intentionally mistreated or hurt another Christian the way I was hurt and mistreated. And if I did, I would try to go back and make it right."

I've wrestled with those feelings. What do you do when reality conflicts with the ideal—when that big chasm of mistrust gapes between you and a brother or sister in Christ? What do you do when the other "siblings" in the family act in a way that doesn't merit trust?

Most of the same dynamics that go on in human families carry over into our spiritual family. There are always people who, like spoiled children, think they should receive preferential treatment because they see themselves as "smarter," "more skilled," "more gifted," "more powerful," "of the preferred sex," or because they wear a badge that says "Leader" on it. They think they have earned the right to better treatment—to more attention, power, prestige, or preference than others. They think they deserve more love. Because you can't earn God's love—it's standard equipment God builds into His relationship with every one of us—they are wrong.

Sarah, a young missionary, observed that on her mission base some people got their way by smooth-talking, by making a big show of looking agreeable. Sarah saw that while these folks gave an appearance of agreement, they were really maneuvering themselves into position to get their own way. Sarah and other straight-talkers who spoke up were penalized by their leaders and told they were "critical," "fault-finders," "full of bitterness." Instead of addressing the real issue of favoritism toward the sweet-talkers, the mission leaders deflected the problem back onto the straight-talkers. That way they wouldn't have to face the fact that the real problem was their own need to be sweet-talked, agreed with, and never challenged. Preferring the "compliant, agreeable child" means that compliance and agreeableness rule the house. This makes for an out-of-order household.

Another example. Ron attended a men's weekend retreat with some other businessmen. Bob, a successful and influential man, was part of the group attending. Ron observed how the retreat leaders scrambled to meet Bob's every desire for comfort and convenience. In short, Bob ruled the spiritual household that weekend, to the disappointment and disgust of the other guys. Whatever was taught from the Scriptures that weekend was drowned out in Ron's mind by the fact that the leaders were violating the biblical principle that preference for the wealthy and successful goes against the spirit of "equal value for all" that must reign in God's family (James 2:1–9).

Others in our new "family" operate by another double standard. When they are at fault they want mercy and forgiveness, and all kinds of allowances to be made for them. But when other people are at fault they pound hard the gavel of justice.

There are other bad dynamics we could talk about here, but I'm aiming at a more basic problem—the fact that double standards exist at all, because that fact means that two sets of rules are at work. We shouldn't expect anything but confusion, willful wrongdoing, and wounding. Relationships always become chaotic when groups or families or individuals enforce rules unevenly.

When the Spirit Reigns

The body of Christ that Paul depicts is more than an organization and more than a collection of people who mentally agree on a set of Bible doctrines. There is a supernatural interrelatedness among people who have a relationship with Jesus Christ. In 1 Corinthians 6 and 14, and in Romans 12, Paul makes these points:

We are members of the same body.

We have diverse gifts.

But we are drawn together and "baptized into one body" by one and the same Spirit (1 Corinthians 12:13).

Because our individualistic culture neglects our corporate oneness I want to repeat a point for emphasis. What these passages say is that there is no longer room to think in terms of you *as an individual totally separate* from me—or worse, you *versus* me. We share a common identity. When we look in a moment at the ramifications of this, you'll understand the breadth and power this truth is meant to have in our lives.

First, I'd like to point out that Christians, in an attempt to make churches "work," have structured church governments in a variety of ways. Christians have also tried to set up pecking orders in church relationships—for instance, on a supposed overruling "hierarchy" of apostles, prophets, evangelists, pastors, and teachers. Christians have also tried to make marriages work by creating "ideal" structures—some of which bear more resemblance to corporate America than a wedding together of two spiritual beings.

What's missing in every one of these approaches? *The Holy Spirit.*

The Spirit breathes life into any construction where people are joined together. When we don't understand how God intends Christians to relate to one another, we almost always create relational connections ripe for misuse, hurt, and destructiveness. We end up with relationships in which one party benefits at the expense of another. When self-centeredness takes over, it's easy to act like a wolf among sheep.

The Spirit's rule—and this rule isn't a law that dominates, but a force that releases life and health and freedom to the body of Christ—is revealed in the New Testament in a series of "one another" statements. We start with the assumption that we have been joined together to learn how to work well together—and here's the important part—*so that every individual part benefits from all the others*. With that fact solidly planted in our heads, we'll see how amazingly practical the "one another" statements are.

Let's take a look at them now.

A Spiritual House Built for "One Another"

The first set of "one anothers" I want to introduce tells us how *not* to treat our spiritual brothers and sisters:

Don't bite and devour one another (Galatians 5:15).

Don't lie to one another (Colossians 3:9).

Don't speak evil of one another (James 4:11).

Don't grumble against one another (James 5:9).

Don't judge one another (Romans 14:3).

If I go against these "one anothers," someone inevitably gets hurt.

The second set of "one anothers" tell us where we can count on help when we need it:

Accept one another (Romans 15:7).

Bear one another's burdens (Galatians 6:2).

Bear with one another, with all humility, gentleness, and patience (Ephesians 4:2).

Be kind to one another, tender-hearted, forgiving one another (Ephesians 4:32).

Confess your sins to one another, and pray for one another (James 5:16).

If I actively do these "one anothers," someone will always be helped.

At a recent workshop a pastor balked when I laid out this list as one means of bringing the life of the Spirit into the body of Christ. In essence his question was, "What about sin?" The words *accepting, bearing burdens*, and *forgiving* made him uncomfortable. He believed that the best help you could give to a Christian struggling with alcoholism or homosexuality, for instance, was to give no help at all. This pastor thought that offering help was the same as giving a person license to continue in their problem. It might even encourage others to jump on the bandwagon and develop the same problem! In his mind, withholding help would act as a deterrent.

Look at how the reasoning would work in a family setting. In that pastor's family of choice, only the so-called "strong" or "smart" kids get help. And only the "healthy" kids get taken to the doctor and dentist. Unfortunately, the unhealthy and weak ones are easily angled away from the flock where they're much easier prey, or they die on the inside while everyone ignores their problem.

The third set of "one anothers" describes interactions with other Christians that build us up.

Pursue what makes for peace and the building up of one another (Romans 14:19).

Have the same kind of care for one another (1 Corinthians 12:25).

Admonish (gently warn) one another (Romans 15:14).

Be devoted to one another, prefer one another when it comes to giving credit (Romans 12:10).

Serve one another (Galatians 5:13).

Submit to one another (Ephesians 5:21).

Regard one another as more important than yourself (Philippians 2:3).

Be hospitable to one another (1 Peter 4:9).

Let me add this important piece to the picture. The Greek word that is translated "one another" is a part of speech that's called a "reciprocal pronoun"—which means that both parties will experience the action being done. If the action is positive—love, support, comfort—*both parties will benefit*. And in the case of negative actions—speaking evil, consuming—*both parties lose*.

The Father's Will That Rules the House

The presence of all these "one anothers" tells us several things.

First of all, God, the Father of this family, wants us involved in each other's lives. Our spiritual relationship with God gives us the foundation for our growth in profound human friendships.

Second, within God's family we need to learn to function in "one another" ways. Learning to work, live, love, and grow together builds on that foundation. Self-sufficiency—whether we are leaders or folks in the pew—makes us useless at joyfully helping meet others' legitimate needs. Sticking together to overcome life's obstacles, in contrast, increases maturity and depth. This is God's design. What a blessing it is when we find relationships like this— *even if we have to stretch to find them.*

I've left one "one another" for last. It's the "one another" that ties all the others together, or that provides the lubricant that keeps us working together when grit gunks up our relationship cogs. It deserves to stand alone.

Love one another.

We are told to love one another in many places throughout the New Testament. But Jesus elevated this "one another" to a status and priority above all the others.

This is My commandment, that you love one another, just as I have loved you (John 15:12).

It is the only "one another" that is earmarked as a *command*. It's as if Jesus, standing in front of His pupils as spiritual teacher, was giving a big wink to signal, "Pay special attention to this one. It's going to be on the test!"

As we noticed earlier, love fulfills the law *and* it accomplishes all the other commands. Love is the "light" in our relationships that will draw others to Christ. It's a witness to the world that He is the One sent from God. And it's even more than that. John says,

> We know that we have passed out of death into life, because we love the brethren (1 John 3:14).

The evidence of love between us is how we can tell that we are spiritually alive. As John adds,

> No one has beheld God at any time; [but] if we love one another, God abides in us, and His love is perfected in us (1 John 4:12).

God is the One building a spiritual house in and through the lives of His children. And He wants to be "seen" by the people who are still in spiritual darkness.

The question is this: Will you and I come out of our *own* blindness? Do we lack a spiritual vision of what God wants to do—far above what our individual lives can accomplish or bear witness— because we wrap up our heads in self-centeredness?

What kind of love for one another will it take to overcome the blindness of people around us caught in materialism and self-centeredness? What will it take to share light with other Christians? And what will it take to bring light to nonbelievers?

No Greater Love Than This

A story I heard the other day gives us a hint. An old man, the story goes, was sitting by a river one day. Watching the water as it moved slowly along the bank, he noticed something floating toward him on the water's surface. As it came closer he saw it was a scorpion struggling helplessly to stay alive. Having a respect for all life, the old man reached out to pluck it from the water.

Instantly the scorpion stung him. The attempt to save its life was obviously perceived as an attack. Still, the old man reached in again and lifted the scorpion to safety. As it rushed away to escape its rescuer, the old man wrapped a handkerchief around his bleeding, painful hand.

A young man who had watched the scene from nearby came over to scoff. "You old fool. Don't you know anything about scorpions? They'll always sting you. That's their nature."

The old man patiently replied, "Yes, I know it's the scorpion's nature to sting. But it's my nature to save the life of any living thing, no matter what it costs."

Greater love has no one than this, that one lay down his life for his friends (John 15:13).

Jesus said that. Jesus, who was God and Man. Shortly thereafter, He returned to His Father's side, where He remains to this day while the Father works out further plans in history.

And now we are His spiritual body on earth. Yes, we *need to be loved*. But we also have a need to *give out love*—to give a love that lays down its life for its friends, even when friends act like scorpions.

The "one anothers" we looked at need to characterize the relationships between Christians, in friendships outside of church buildings and in fellowship gatherings inside church. The degree to which this kind of love, respect, and support exists in our relationships is the degree to which people's sins, problems, needs, pains, and struggles will be touched and healed. No doubt the healing and support will not be perfect, because the church is not God. But God wants to make His living and active presence known through us—His family.

Going Back, or Going On?

I have laid out a high vision of the church. I realize that.

In part, I give this higher view because it's painfully easy to lose sight of what God has in mind for His body when other Christians misuse something as high and holy as a relationship with a brother or sister in Christ. Yet we can't escape the Bible's high vision of the church. When Paul wrote to the Corinthians—who were busily polluting their own fellowship—he painted an image of the church that goes far above the seamy underside of church life that we sooner or later see when a collection of fallen humans comes together. He wanted to open up their understanding to God's higher purposes—and that's what I have meant to do for you as well.

My second reason for taking time to re-create this view of the church is to go a step further on a point we touched on in the last chapter. For the Christian, healing and growth must take place *in the body of Christ*.

It may be that you've put some distance between yourself and other Christians for the present. But what about your future—what does it look like? If you're thinking about playing the role of "the Lone Christian," put that idea out of your head. It won't work. Healing from relationship disasters comes by learning what went wrong the first time—by overcoming our natural withdrawal from pain, to allow us to protect the wounded spot. Does your future look like *more* isolation? Or do you look forward to restoration to healthy, whole relationships?

A rider thrown from a horse only overcomes his or her fear of being thrown by getting back on a horse. Notice that I didn't say it has to be the *same* horse. Realistically, some churches and some relationships may not ever be safe for us to go back to. In some cases we may never see an offender "bring forth fruit in keeping with your repentance," as Jesus put it (Matthew 3:8). A demonstrated willingness to change is the one thing that shows us an offender's heart has been softened. You may need to move on to another church or to another friendship in order to begin growing again. But if that's so, by all means do it!

Yet, as we noted earlier, sometimes you will choose to lay down your life for a friend—or a church—once you've grown enough spiritually not to be wounded again. This can only happen with a specific calling from God—a sense of peace and confidence and inner knowing that no one can force us into a tough situation by a cardboard insistence that "it's the Christian thing to do." Unless you have seen significant growth within yourself, unless the power dynamics that caused the breakdown have changed, spare yourself further grief.

So far, we have focused mainly on damage caused by the *actions* of other Christians. As we have seen, these actions can be very painful and destructive.

But we need to turn our attention next to damage caused by the *inaction* of others—those times when we have urgent needs and other Christians leave us to suffer alone. What we will look at is in some ways even more deadly, a creeping illness causing atrophy and loss to the body of Christ.

4

When Those Who "Care" Are Not There

Being neglected hurts. Neglect is a passive form of inflicting harm, which despite its nonaggressive nature leaves long-lasting damage.

The news media and the courts these days overflow with cases of neglected or abandoned children. The world recognizes that children must be raised in an environment where a responsible adult notices their needs and helps meet them. When basic physical needs go unmet, children get sick and die. When emotional needs are ignored, children grow up socially impaired and can become a menace to themselves and society.

The world sees those needs. But do we as Christians recognize the damage caused in the body of Christ and in the lives of individual Christians when *we* ignore real needs?

Unfortunately, we don't notice needs often enough. As we have noted, some churches feel their only task is to be sure people come to understand the Bible and certain doctrines. "Let God take it from there," or "we're done"—this seems to be the attitude. Too often, though, when someone in one of these churches has real needs, the only help he or she gets is, "Well, you know what the Bible says. . . ."

Other churches, and the Christians they nurture, think their God-given job is to set standards for Christian behavior—like soul-winning or dress codes—and then to monitor each individual's ability to live up to those standards. When a needy person seeks help in one of these churches, there's a good chance they will hear things like, "You should get your mind off your own troubles. Get busy and begin to obey God by doing for others." Or, "How's your prayer life?" Or, "Have you been reading your Bible?" Or, "Maybe your need is an indication that there's sin in your life."

Of course there's an incredible variety in church life. There is the "church as social club," where relationships form around a certain standard of income or lifestyle. Needs and needy people don't look good or fit well in socially oriented churches. There are "traditional churches," where relationships form around the rehearsing (over and over again) of a liturgy or other traditional forms of "worship." Needs and needy people don't fit well into settings where tidy traditions are elevated over the life of flesh-and-blood, in-your-face people. They're grit in the gears of the machinery.

I've spent a good bit of time in the opening chapters pointing out that your need to recover from wounds caused by other Christians will best be met among other Christians. Working out relationships will benefit you *and* the body of Christ, as well. But from this point on I want to focus more directly on the real dangers of letting hurts go untended in order to rouse you to reach out for help and make your needs known. Ultimately, only you can take those first steps to healing.

It's sad but true—many things can take over the life of a church that have little to do with building the *lives* of people. Add to that leaders who for whatever reasons don't notice human need or who feel inhibited by a lack of know-how. All of it adds up to neglect of human needs—when helping to meet people's needs is a great way to help them meet the caring heart of God. And all the time a church can look fairly good from the outside, full of nice people—while on the inside, people suffer because inner needs are neglected.

They Must Be Wonderful Christians, Just Look at Those Big Smiles

My friend Nancy told me her story of growing up in a wonderful church with a wonderful spiritual heritage—yet saw her inner needs almost entirely overlooked.

For her entire childhood Nancy's family attended the same church in central North Dakota. It was an independent, fundamental, Bible-believing, soul-winning, sin-hating, separated church. Right across the street (and there are only a few streets in that town of two hundred people) was another independent, fundamental, Bible-believing, soul-winning, sin-hating, separated church. But the churches never got together because there was a doctrine or two on which the pastors disagreed. Folks in Nancy's church were more doctrinally pure. The people across the street were suspect.

Nancy's great-grandfather, a legend in their church, had been the pastor forever. He had gotten off a boat from Scandinavia in New York harbor, ridden on horseback to North Dakota, climbed off the horse and preached in the same church for the next forty years. One Christmas Eve, after delivering his message, he sat down in one of the five huge oak chairs up on the platform. And right there in front of everyone, he died. Like Enoch, the Lord took him and he was no more. His life and his death rocketed him to legendary status.

His son Emil, Nancy's great-uncle, became the pastor after him. He led the church for about thirty years, then he died. Nancy, grown up and relocated by this time, returned for the funeral to support her cousin Mary, Emil's only daughter.

At the close of the funeral, a special tape was played of Emil singing and playing the piano during a Sunday night service many years before. As he sang he sobbed so hard he could hardly get through the song.

> What a friend we have in Jesus,
> all our sins and griefs to bear.
> What a privilege to carry
> everything to God in prayer. . . .

By the end, there wasn't a dry eye in the place. While growing up, Nancy had watched Uncle Emil play, sing, and sob that song at least twice a year, every year for twenty years. She remembered listening as a child and wondering what it must be like to love Jesus so much—and know He loves *you* so much—you can't even sing about it without crying.

After the service, Nancy went with her cousin Mary over to Emil's house. A lifetime of personal effects needed sorting and, in her grief, Mary could use the help. In fact, Emil had kept many of his wife's personal things after she died, so the job turned out to be much bigger than either of them anticipated.

At one point the two women went down into the basement. And there, stuffed under the stairwell in a hole under the floor, they found boxes of pornographic material, some of it the over-the-counter variety and some of real hard-core content.

When Nancy related the story to me she broke down in tears. "Mary and I were absolutely wrecked by the whole thing—not to mention the rest of the family. I felt so sad, and I needed to talk to someone. I thought you would understand." She paused, and another emotion swept across her face. "I'm *angry* too! Because there just isn't anywhere to go with a problem like that when you're in a church that's that *holy*."

And I thought to myself, *Yes there is. You go to the basement.*

I too feel sad about what Mary and Nancy discovered, because sexual compulsions and sins are a common problem among people in the ministry. It's one of the most common problems in the church. I feel sad that there was no help for Emil in his own church. In its holiness, rightness, judgmentalism, and zeal for "the lost," the church had let Emil down. All that counted, it seems, was that Emil and his family showed up every Sunday, smiles pasted on their faces, looking on the outside like a wonderful Christian family. Outward image and outward behavior were everything. They had neglected the most important part.

The condition and needs of the heart.

God's Unsettling Desire

Early one Sunday morning, I turned on the television and came across a preacher who was expounding up and down Revelation, chapter 3.

The way this man handled the Scripture—about God's warning to one church, in Laodicea—made me think about Emil's church, where an outward show of faith was all you needed to look good.

> And to the angel of the church in Laodicea write: The Amen, the faithful and true Witness, the Beginning of the creation of God, says this: "I know your deeds, that you are neither cold nor hot; I would that you were cold or hot. So because you are lukewarm, and neither hot nor cold, I will spit you out of My mouth" (vv. 14–16).

His application mimicked every other preacher I've ever heard teach that passage. A *hot* Christian is someone who comes to church every time the doors open, gives a lot of money, and volunteers personal time sacrificially. He insinuated that there are degrees of "hotness"—a kind of "thermal hierarchy" of the faithful.

Missionaries are the hottest. Then others in full-time service, followed by dedicated volunteers, involved laypeople. And then other primates.

The category of *cold* actually contains two subcategories of people. The first consists of non-Christians; severely "backslidden" believers comprise the second. These Christians are involved in the whole gamut of worldly activities, from going to bars to participating in the most heinous, immoral, and violent of behaviors.

Mediocre believers make up the last category, the *lukewarm*. Happy to have Jesus as Savior, they haven't made Him Lord of their lives. And he listed many of the outward activities that make up a life—work, hobbies, possessions.

As I listened to that preacher, I considered—perhaps more deeply than ever before—the implications of his message. I could understand why God would prefer people to be in the *hot* category—if, in fact, hotness is measured by outward performance. But the text seems to indicate that *cold* is desirous to God, too. Could this be true? Would He really rather people be *cold* instead of *lukewarm*? That would mean God's stance is more favorable toward people with no faith in Him than toward those whose faith is middling. And it would mean that God can better tolerate those who kill, rape, and flaunt their unbelief than the legions of average, bored pew-sitters.

The more I mulled over what I'd heard the more confused I became.

Not long afterward I received a letter from a man who had read *The Subtle Power of Spiritual Abuse*. He had been helped by the book and was writing to offer his thanks. The bulk of the letter, however, centered on his thoughts concerning the above text. He heard it explained in basically the same way as I had, with an emphasis on good works, bad works, and few works. His questions were essentially the same as mine. What does it mean to be *hot* for the Lord? ("On fire," as the saying goes.) What does it mean to be *cold*? Or *lukewarm*? Are these things measured by emotional fervor? Good works?

Or was the Spirit of God pointing the Laodiceans to something else?

This man's insights and my subsequent studies of the passage helped me to see this passage in an entirely new light.

First, I discovered that the "temperature" references refer to a natural phenomenon in the region—a hot springs outside Laodicea that flowed through the city on its way to the sea. This piece of knowledge makes quite a bit of difference in your reading of the passage.

The water near Hierapolis was famous for its hot springs. Thermal water bubbled out of the ground and formed pools believed to possess healing qualities. The sick or wounded would travel great distances to bathe in the curative hot waters. From Hierapolis a system of aqueducts conveyed the waters to Laodicea. And after the water left Laodicea it eventually flowed into the ocean. The closer to its final destination, the cooler it became. It reached its coolest temperature just before it spilled into the sea. It was at this point that tired or hot travelers could drink the water and be refreshed. For drinking purposes, then, the farther from Laodicea the better.

Second, the confrontation in Revelation 3 is directed at the "church in Laodicea." The Spirit of God was not talking to Bill, Sally, Joe, or Bonnie. He was writing to *that church.*

Putting these two factors together can help us understand the true and full weight of this particular confrontation. It seems that the church in Laodicea was not a "hot" place where people who were sick or wounded could find healing. Neither was it a "cold" place where those who were hot or tired could find rest and refreshment. Christ's body in Laodicea was "lukewarm," providing no benefit to the afflicted and weary.

Churches that are lukewarm aren't harmful in an aggressive sense. It's not that they do damage—it's just that they aren't useful. They don't really *help* anyone. And so, it seems, they are distasteful to God.

Getting Around Some "Cold" Christians

A woman I'll call Betty once came into the church office and asked my secretary if there was someone she could talk to. She'd never been to the church, but she was in the middle of a crisis with her son and didn't know what to do. As it happened, I was between counseling sessions, so my secretary asked her to wait while she checked with me.

In a few moments I went to meet the woman and I found her sound asleep in a chair. Looking at her, I thought, *If she is so tired and stressed-out that she can't stay awake at 12:30 in the afternoon sitting straight up in a chair, sleep is probably what she needs most right now.*

I left the room and let her sleep. At the end of this "session," I awakened her and made an appointment to see her the next day.

When we met, I found out that she had a son whose alcohol use was out of control. He was coming in at all hours, stealing money from her, bringing home sex partners, and giving away things from her house to his friends. Her husband had headed for Alaska with another woman and left her with several months' bills to pay for rent, car insurance, and utilities. The saddest part was that the church she attended, from which she was renting her house, had just given her two weeks' notice to move out. Why? The elders had decided that she was a poor mother and had failed to control her nineteen-year-old son, who was still technically under her "spiritual umbrella of authority." Throwing her out was their idea of church discipline for her "sin."

I excused myself and went into another office to make a phone call to the Bennetts, a couple in our church who I knew had an extra room. They are also among the most laid-back, gracious, and hospitable people I know. I asked if they could temporarily provide a safe, restful environment for someone I was counseling. They were more than happy to help Betty out.

When I returned and offered Betty this couple's extra room, she seemed overwhelmed. After an embarrassing moment of hemming and hawing she accepted. There really wasn't much else she could do. Then I gave her three referrals: first, to a career counselor who could help her begin to find ways to become financially responsible for herself; second, to a counselor who could help her work through the grief of all the losses that had crashed in on her, and to set up healthy boundaries with her son; and third, to a support group in our church, because she was experiencing the painful effects of loving a person who was chemically dependent.

Betty's life changed dramatically in a very short time. She "clicked" with the Bennetts. (You'd have to be a Hell's Angel not to, and even then . . .) In one week, she looked like a completely different human being. She found a job and rented her own apartment. And in a short time, without Betty's unhelpful help to prop him up, the son's lifestyle crashed. Soon he got real help himself.

Comfort one another. Be kind to one another. Bear one another's burdens. Receive one another. Be hospitable to one another.

Have compassion for one another. Serve one another. Love one another.

Folks, helping people in their need is not complicated.

An interesting sidenote to Betty's story: Not long after this all came down, a man from Betty's former church ran into her at a shopping mall. He marveled at how great she looked, because the last time he saw her she looked pretty tired. He had wondered where she had disappeared to and was concerned for her. She told him about the experience with her son and husband and how the church elders responded. She then shared about the Bennetts, her new job, her support group, even the nap in the office. The man felt sad and angry that she had experienced that kind of treatment at the hands of their church leaders.

Later, I learned, this man made an appointment to meet with the leaders of his church to confront them about what happened to Betty. When they met, he told them about the care she had received at our church—Church of the Open Door. One of the elders angrily leaped out of his seat and bellowed, "I am sick and tired of hearing about Church of the Open *Sore.* All they do is minister to sick people!"

I take the intended insult as a compliment.

I haven't told this story to position myself and Open Door over other Christians, or to say, "Boy, aren't we Christlike!" I share this because of the truly sad point of the story: Betty *could* have gotten help at this other church, because God has placed the people and resources there. I look at this church, and others, and it's like looking at wonderful hospital facilities—except that the orderlies, nurses, and physicians are wandering around seemingly oblivious to the amazing tools of healing that lie right within their grasp.

Are You the Christ?

Luke gives us an instructive clue about Jesus and something central to His ministry:

> The scroll of the prophet Isaiah was handed to him. Unrolling it, he found the place where it is written: "The Spirit of the Lord is on me, because he has anointed me to preach good news to the poor. He has sent me to proclaim freedom for the prisoners and recovery of sight for the blind, to release the oppressed, to proclaim the year of the Lord's favor." Then he rolled

up the scroll, gave it back to the attendant and sat down. The eyes of everyone in the synagogue were fastened on him, and he began by saying to them, "Today this scripture is fulfilled in your hearing" (Luke 4:17–21, NIV).

This carpenter was claiming, in front of a hometown crowd, that He fulfilled the prophecy in Isaiah 61. Actually, there is more to the prophecy. In addition to the part that Jesus quoted, Isaiah includes binding up the brokenhearted, proclaiming freedom to prisoners, comforting all who mourn, restoring a spirit of praise instead of a spirit of fainting.

The elders in Nazareth had an interesting response to Jesus' incredible claim. First, they wondered about Him, "Isn't this Joseph's son?" Then they tried to throw Him off a cliff.

Jesus left Nazareth and traveled around for some time, doing the very things found in that prophecy. Then He got a different kind of response.

When John heard in prison what Christ was doing, he sent his disciples to ask him, "Are you the one who was to come, or should we expect someone else?" (Matthew 11:2–3, NIV)

John the Baptist, who had heard the voice from heaven when he baptized Jesus, now wondered if Jesus was *really* the Messiah. John, like everyone else in Israel, had expected a military Messiah who would run the Romans out of town. Instead, they got a teacher. A healer. A lover. There was no military vindication of the Jewish people, no outward exaltation of the delivering power of their God. Had John put his life on the line for the right person? If he was checking his expectations against reality, who could blame him? What was the work of the Messiah supposed to look like?

Jesus' response to John's disciples was something like this: "You've got it right, boys. Go tell John that this is what the Messiah is about. . . ." And then He quoted the Isaiah 61 prophecy once again, as well as other prophecies in Isaiah—all having to do with healing and the restoration of the soul of mankind.

Are You the *Body* of Christ?

Should the body of Christ care about the same kinds of things as Jesus? Should we be involved in the same compassionate healing, comforting, and restoring work as Jesus?

One woman who contacted me recently told how she had asked her church for their help and support to overcome wounds from her past. She was told, "Don't look back. Look what happened to Lot's wife."

She had gone to these people as the body of Christ, and their reply said, "We have nothing hopeful to tell the afflicted. The brokenhearted are still brokenhearted. The captives are still imprisoned. No one has experienced forgiveness. We have no comfort for the mourners. There are no sounds of gladness or praise."

I would like to paraphrase John the Baptist's question, on behalf of the needy who approach Christ's body seeking help: *Is this the body of Christ, or shall we look for another?*

In light of the neglect so many Christians have experienced in church, I believe this is a legitimate question.

Returning to Uncle Emil—and You

What was Great-Uncle Emil crying about when he sang about Jesus? Nancy had thought he was overwhelmed by his love for Jesus, and Jesus' love for him. I wonder.

I have seen people wrestling with sexual problems—people who love Jesus and know He loves them—cry because they know that loving Jesus doesn't make these problems disappear. I have seen people cry because of the agony and exhaustion they carry from extolling the virtues of Christian living on Sunday yet living another way the rest of the week. I have seen people cry because of the desperate loneliness that results from hiding their life from the people most important to them.

And people like Betty cry because there is no help to be found in the "Jesus" represented by their church.

Great-Uncle Emil—legend and son of a legend—was alone in his own kind of prison. We could also paraphrase John the Baptist's question to read: "Emil, in the prison of his sexual compulsion, having heard the works of (fill in the blank with the name of a church), asked, 'Are you really Christ's body, or shall I look for another?' "

If those who were supposed to care have not been there for you in your need, I'm truly sorry for you. Neglect hurts. If a serious emotional need is ignored long enough—if there is no safe place to run for help—it will impair your whole life. If you have genuine need for material help and support, it's hard to listen to sermons and Bible studies while you're overwhelmed by financial despair.

I am encouraging you here to continue seeking help, support, and encouragement until your need is resolved. No church will solve your needs *for* you—but healthy churches will support you as you seek the resolution you need. No healthy church will ever belittle you or make you feel guilty for *having* the need. No healthy church will counsel you to ignore the need until it goes away.

In the end, you may have to search for a time until you find a setting where you're supported and encouraged. You may have to reach out to some new Christian friends.

Yet I can assure you, God's caring people *are* there. And when you find them they will be refreshing, healing waters to you. Whether you find them in your church or another, let these people become *the* church to you.

5

Wounded by Friendly Fire

It was impossible to avoid the story that broke onto the international scene in late 1993—the sad story of Olympic figure-skaters Tonya Harding and Nancy Kerrigan.

As you may recall, during the competition for a national figure-skating championship in Detroit, Nancy Kerrigan was bashed in the knee by an assailant. Her wounded knee would have kept her out of the Olympics had it not been for the care of competent professionals—not to mention a lot of hard work by Kerrigan, plus the support of friends and family.

After some investigation, Tonya Harding's security staff and her ex-husband were identified as conspirators in a plot to knock Kerrigan out of the competition. Further investigations and a media-feeding frenzy brought us the revelation that Harding herself was possibly connected to the attack. Did she mastermind the scheme? Did she know about it ahead of time—and if so, why didn't she stop it? Eventually, Harding was implicated, enraging the world.

Wounding is all the more outrageous when it comes from someone supposedly on your side. Harding had been willing to harm an Olympic teammate for her own personal gain—a shocking betrayal.

Members of the same team are supposed to have the same motives. A "team spirit" rules as the players work united toward one goal. In the Olympics, when one team member employs his or her skills well, the whole team advances. Granted, everyone knows that two skaters on the same team do compete against each other for Olympic medals. But Kerrigan surely did not expect destructive motives to undercut the uplifting motives that power individuals to work for the good of a whole team—a "team-spiritedness."

The body of Christ isn't a place for individuals to aggrandize themselves, their personal ambitions, their unhealthy needs, or their dreams of glory. It's a series of human relationships aimed at one and the same goal: to help bring others into a stronger knowledge of Jesus Christ, and to empower them to help others with the knowledge and help they have received.

Yet many Christians are scraped and bruised when they bump up against motives that have little or nothing to do with the true spiritual goals of the body of Christ. I find it odd—and kind of maddening, too—that it is often the people with the best and purest motives who are accused of wrongdoing. And their accusers turn out to be the ones who, upon investigation, operate out of selfish and self-aggrandizing motives. Or the accusations come from people who are so blind that they can't see the simple good that good people are trying to accomplish—it's hard to understand *how* they can be so blind.

I think of this phenomenon as being wounded by "friendly fire." While one Christian is working hard to do something good and worthwhile, he gets shot in the back by other spiritual soldiers who are supposed to be working for the same cause—while, actually, other motives are at work.

A Spiritual "Oxymoron"

The other day I was doing some work at a copy center near my home. As I went to the cashier to pay my bill, I noticed a sign above the cash register: Original Reproductions. I thought, *How can that be? Either something is original, or it's a reproduction.*

There's a name for that kind of phrase—it's an "oxymoron," which is a phrase containing words that contradict each other. I like oxymorons—in fact, I collect them. *Military intelligence* is one of my dad's favorites. I like to laugh at *sanitary landfill. Jumbo shrimp. Reverend Jeff VanVonderen.* . . . As you can see, some oxymorons are humorous.

But some are not. "Wounded by friendly fire" is an oxymoron that holds no humor. I had heard the phrase many times, but didn't feel the impact of it until the Gulf War in 1991. During a recap of one day's events, a newsperson used the phrase to describe how several American soldiers had become the latest casualties of the fighting. I had become intimately familiar with that conflict, as I was flat on my back during most of it, recuperating from surgery to repair a ruptured disc. The pain in my back and left leg was still quite excruciating. But I remember how my back pain was eclipsed by the sick feeling in my stomach when I heard the phrase and realized what it meant to someone's mom and dad ... to a young wife somewhere, with small children.

And many times since then, I have felt that twinge in my stomach when I think about "friendly fire" that slams into Christians every day. The spiteful words and actions that send Christians reeling.

What does "friendly fire" look like in the body of Christ? Here are a few "news clips" that may make you as sad as they make me:

Laura poured out her heart and soul as the volunteer director of the church choir. After two years of sacrificing personal time to bless her church, she was invited to a vestry meeting—where she was blasted with a volley of criticism and accusations. She was "intentionally" ignoring the older people by using too many contemporary songs. She was favoring some soloists over others. And, by the way, was she up front to be noticed by the men, or to direct the choir? Some of those skirts could be a little longer.

Dave wanted to get a men's prayer group together. An elder in his church accused him of "pushing an agenda" and "trying to start a faction."

Louisa serves in a ministry that occasionally holds all-night prayer meetings. It's quietly assumed that staff members will show up when the ministry leader calls for all-night prayer, or when overtime work is needed—even though that was never spelled out before Louisa joined the ministry, and even though she receives no salary but rather raises her own support. Louisa wants to give all that she can give of herself to the ministry. But she wonders where the boundary lies between being allowed to make choices and having the choices made for her. Recently, the ministry founder let her know that she was "obviously not committed to serving the Lord" because she wasn't "one-hundred-percent committed to this ministry."

Bill was an elder who felt his church would be better off building an addition to their facility instead of making massive efforts to build a new church. Why not use the money to fund ministries from the church into the surrounding community? He was accused of having a *holier-than-thou* attitude. "If you have so little understanding of what this church needs and where it's headed, Bill," said the pastor, "maybe it's time for you to resign. I came here to build a big church."

Every one of these folks has served God with an honest, giving heart—and yet *their motives* were being used against them, or rather, someone's mistaken judgment of their motives.

To these people, the most painful thing was discovering that other Christians could accuse them when they were intent on doing good—and that their accusers could have such self-seeking motives and not even see it in themselves.

What motive are we supposed to bring to our relationships and our service?

In 2 Corinthians 5:20, the apostle Paul calls us "ambassadors" for Christ. That means we are to be men and women who beg the world on His behalf to be reconciled to God. An ambassador is the representative of one country to another. He or she resides in a building called an "embassy," which is usually found in some kind of compound. Even though the embassy and compound are located in the host country, they are actually an extension of the visiting country. In other words, when you're in an embassy of the United States of America, you have literally stamped on American soil.

That's especially good to know if hostilities flare between the host and visiting countries. As a citizen in a hostile country, outside of your country's embassy you are in unfriendly, unsafe territory. Inside you are, in all respects, on safe terrain. This situation remains until the two countries are reconciled.

The church—the whole body of believers—is God's embassy in the world, the safe place in the midst of the unsafe place. Believers are His ambassadors. Our goal here in "wolf" territory is to represent the existence of a better world—to be beacons of hope to the oppressed citizens of this world. (See Matthew 6.) And for our own tired, disoriented, or endangered fellow-citizens, we provide safe conduct out of danger and into a place of rest and protection.

An Unsafe Embassy

In the last chapter we saw how believers are let down when

God's people neglect one another. Neglecting to "bear one another's burdens" results in having to carry the weight of your problems by yourself. Failing to "comfort one another" leaves believers by themselves in their uncomforted state. We miss out on experiencing the healing of forgiveness when we don't "confess our sins to one another" and "pray for one another." Because of neglect, wounded believers stay wounded. And they feel alone as well.

Here we are considering the result when other "ambassadors" who appear to be representing the kingdom are actually driven by lesser core motives. What happens when our "embassy"—that is, the people assigned by the Holy Spirit to provide safe conduct out of danger—actually perpetrate our wounds? It's one thing to go in the front door of "The Church That Love Built" and not experience love—to have wounds inflicted by people and circumstances go untended. It's quite another to be drawn to that church by the promise of love and then to be treated like an enemy or second-class citizen. It's outrageous. Yet this great tragedy is exactly what many people have experienced.

Let's take a look at the dynamics of Christians being "wounded by friendly fire."

I have pored over the responses I've gotten to *Tired of Trying to Measure Up* and *The Subtle Power of Spiritual Abuse*. I have listened to countless stories of people attacked by others in the church. And in those stories I have noticed that three main relationship dynamics inflict most of the wounds experienced by the people of God: lack of honesty, lack of acceptance, and lack of honor.

We'll take the rest of this chapter to focus on the first dynamic—how people are hurt when they aren't treated with honesty. In the following chapter we'll look at the ways people are hurt when members of God's family act superior to one another, or when they play favorites.

Lack of Honesty

Ephesians 4:25 says:

> Therefore, laying aside falsehood, speak truth, each one of you, with his neighbor, for we are members of one another.

Please notice that there are three instructions contained in this verse.

The first is that we are to lay aside—to aggressively cast off—falsehood. This is reiterated in Colossians 3:9, "Do not lie to one another."

The second is the exhortation to "speak truth." Literally, this says, "Speak forth only of every truth." (This same idea is found also in Zechariah 8:16–17 and Ephesians 4:15.) The third instruction is to direct these actions to our "neighbor" or to one another. When we are derelict in any of these responsibilities, our false-speaking inevitably causes hurts.

Here's an excerpt from a letter I received recently from a Canadian named Peter:

> Having analyzed my own disastrous experiences over and over, I have found a common denominator. In all the negative church experiences I have had, gossip and slander were at the root of it. It seems that nobody takes very seriously the scriptural mandate to take offenses directly to the suspected offender first.

In that brief paragraph Peter reports several ways in which Ephesians 4:25 has not been heeded. The result for him was the destruction of relationships and enormous personal disappointment.

Gossip

The first destructive force is gossip. Gossip is *talking about*, instead of *talking to* one another. The Greek work for gossip is *phluaros*, and comes from a word that means "to bubble," and means "to tattle." A gossip is a tattletale.

If a little girl tattles on another child, she usually isn't reporting falsely. If she was, it wouldn't be called tattling; it would be called lying. She tells the truth, but tells it to the wrong person, usually to try to get the second person to take her side or to intervene on her behalf. This alleviates her frustration with a situation, yet someone else has to do the hard work she should be doing. When this happens at our house we say, "You need to talk to your (dad/sister/mom) about that." Sometimes people think their motives are innocent—"I just wanted to see what you think about the situation."

Gossip usually happens one to one. But sometimes it happens in a public setting, which is even more humiliating for the one being "bubbled" about. This can be seen in another letter I received:

> In the [church] we eventually left, people—even the lead-

ers—gather information on each other. They learn of woundings and weaknesses in one another's lives. Then if someone questions or disagrees, all the information is dragged out. They are even preached against from the pulpit. When this happened to me I asked the pastor why he humiliated me in front of everyone. He said the Holy Spirit was "leading him" to do it this way.

I can't imagine that God is too happy about getting credit for gossip, because what this pastor did cannot be sugar-coated or elevated by calling it something else. God has clear instructions for us if we have genuine concern about something in another believer's life. Romans 15:14 says, "Admonish [mildly warn] one another." Speak gently to the person you're concerned about.

Slander

The second destructive force mentioned in Peter's letter is slander. Like gossip, slander is *talking about* instead of *talking to*. But unlike the gossip, the slanderer spreads *untruths*. The Hebrew language paints graphic pictures of the concept of slander. In Proverbs 10:18 the word translated *slander* means "to glide slowly and intentionally." In Ezekiel 22:9 the word means "to travel about carrying tales." The Greek word is *katalalos* and means "backbiting," "whispering," "speaking evil of," or "defaming."

In 2 Corinthians 12:20, Paul says he fears that when he returns to Corinth he will find slander there. First Peter 2:1 tells us to lay it aside. James 4:11 says, "Don't do it." And in Psalm 101:5 we get a glimpse of what God thinks: "Whoever secretly slanders his neighbor, him I will destroy."

Lied to, or not told the truth

With this last destructive dynamic, the "one another" part is right. This is *talking to* the right person, not *talking about* him to someone else. But "don't lie, do tell the truth," is what Ephesians 4:25 says. Many Christians find themselves lied to—or at least communicated to sideways, in a manner that shields the truth. You would think that relating to each other straightforwardly wouldn't be that hard, and that the importance of relating to one another with honesty and openness would be pretty obvious. You would not believe all of the rationalizations I have heard—many from pastors who justify lying to people, or at least not telling them the truth:

"It's for their own good."

"It's too late for them to change."

"Honor your father and your mother."

"They couldn't handle it if I told them the truth."

"It's the *southern* way." (northern, western, and eastern, too, it seems!)

"It wouldn't do any good."

"Touch not the Lord's anointed."

And the list goes on.

Nevertheless, false-speaking is unbelievably harmful. Lying to someone violates their trust. Acting like you can't tell someone the truth is treating them like they aren't capable, that they're fortunate to have you around to protect them from finding out what's real. This is a condescending, discounting way to act toward one another.

In addition, one of the seven abominations God hates in Proverbs 6:16–19 is "a lying tongue." And in Proverbs 12:22 Solomon says, "Lying lips are an abomination to the LORD, but those who deal *faithfully* are His delight." That we as believers shouldn't be willing to compromise the truth can be seen further in the fact that Paul calls the church "the pillar and support of the truth" (1 Timothy 3:15).

Gossip, slander, lying, hiding the truth—all these are unhealthy ways of communicating disrespect and humiliating others. All circumvent the building of true relationships. All hurt others by damaging reputations and betraying trust. They leave Christians—especially those who refuse to resort to the same tactics—feeling helpless to defend themselves, like they're tied to the tracks in front of a runaway train of damaging information. Laura, Dave, Bill, Louisa, Peter—all were harmed by Christians who wouldn't talk to them directly about misinterpreted motives, people who recruited others to their gossipy or slanderous viewpoint before they launched their attack. This is not Christian—not even the work of mature, healthy adults. It is sin, and has wolf tracks all over it.

These behaviors miss God's mark for healthy communication in relationships. Instead of building a sense of family, they tear people down and force people to choose sides. And in the place of community there are conspiracies.

In the next chapter we will examine how Christians are hurt when others in the body of Christ degrade them.

6

Preference Instead of Deference

I was born and raised in a community of six hundred people in northeastern Wisconsin. For most people in my home area, church was an important part of life. My family attended an independent Baptist church in town, about two miles from our home. Like many churches, ours was hyper-conservative and legalistic.

What I mean by that is the *idea* of God's grace was frequently tossed around in the pulpit and in Sunday school classes. But our real acceptance by God and by other Christians was actually based on behaviors deemed "spiritual" by church authorities. God's "yes" toward you was called into question if your actions didn't measure up to the religious standards of our group.

They seldom did.

These standards went past Scripture's call to morality, generosity, kindness, and faith. They included the length of your hair, the college you attended, your preferred version of the Bible, the people with whom you were friends, and how you spent your Sunday afternoons. "Spirituality" wrapped itself in behavior and attitudes, which were anti-intellectual, anti-technology, anti-communist, anti-Catholic, anti-black, anti-Jew, anti-female, anti-lots-of-stuff. Loving America was equated with loving God. Jesus was a white Anglo-Saxon Protestant who spoke King James English, hated Russians, and sported a butch haircut.

The psyche of our church owed much to the fact that it was basically a family-run operation. The people who wielded power in that church were members of the same family, or at least people

77

of whom they approved. The ruling elite consisted of a set of parents, several daughters and sons and their spouses. This cadre held most of the key board and committee positions in the church, contributed the most money, and dominated the agenda and conversation at any church function.

Once, as a seven-year-old, I went forward to accept Jesus Christ as my personal Savior and Lord after a particularly scary message at Vacation Bible School. I didn't know *exactly* what that meant— but what I did know for sure was that I didn't want to go to hell. Hell had just been vividly described to us as a place of "utter loneliness where you never saw another human being for the rest of eternity. And you would be in indescribable agony from the heat, so that even if you did see someone you'd keep as far away from them as possible—so they wouldn't touch your smoldering flesh (I guess) by accident."

If I have to eat my seven-year-old pride to go up the aisle in front of everyone and parrot a prayer for some mean-sounding guy in order to avoid the lake of fire, I'll do it!

Looking back I don't think my "conversion" had anything to do with Jesus. I don't believe I became a Christian. What I did become was a person who—from age seven until sometime later—*acted* like a Christian. Why? To protect the hearty approval I received from that summer day's performance.

In this sterile environment—characterized by conditional approval and acceptance—it was not okay to question or struggle. In fact, being on top spiritually, physically, and doctrinally was all that mattered. As you can imagine, the struggles of an adolescent boy were particularly difficult in that setting. But I wondered about the world outside my little religious cocoon. I marveled at the changes that were transforming my own body and the bodies of those around me. There were a few of my girl friends whom I would rather had been my *girlfriends*. But my awakening sexuality and intellect threatened to get me "disfellowshiped," so I lived like a spiritual secret agent—living one life when people were looking, another when they weren't.

An Island of Acceptance

During this time there was a couple, Hank and Lois, who were the youth sponsors at our church. They were the only people, except my own family, from whom I experienced any degree of love and acceptance. The irony in this is that they were members of the ruling family. They seemed to approach life and relationships in a way that made me wonder if twenty years before one of the family's biological babies had been switched at birth with someone from a nice family. These people had a sense of humor. They had fun. They weren't sourpusses. Who were these people?

Don't get me wrong. They were still very legalistic and uptight about things like dress-code and reading only the "right Bible." But I was desperate for acceptance, and they were a couple of notches closer to normal.

Hank spent a lot of time with me. We went fishing, hunting, and snowmobiling. We talked about more than the Second Coming of Christ or how wrong beliefs goofed up people. We talked about "stuff." This guy was on to me, though. He knew what a sneaky, insincere people-pleaser I was. He knew what a dangerous double-agent I was with the opposite sex. He and Lois were worried about me. And they prayed for me a lot.

Upon graduation from high school, I was off to college. Over the next few years I made one wrong choice after another. Without the external environment to pressure me positively, I simply conformed my untransformed self to the negative circumstances that surrounded me. Put a people-pleaser in a negative environment and the results are disastrous. But as David says, "God's arm was not short." After a series of failures and painful lifestyle-related consequences, I crashed and burned. And in the ashes of my life I found a relationship with Jesus Christ.

Several years afterward I remembered Hank and Lois with gratitude. But one result of my headlong dash to ditch my early church environment and anything associated with it was that I lost contact with them. While I hadn't known it as a teen, I had since learned the apparent reason why Hank and Lois were different. They knew what it was to struggle. They had gotten pregnant before marriage. I can only imagine the pain and shame they experienced in this *image-is-everything* church, family, and village. Perhaps it was their pain that produced the understanding and tolerance I had experienced.

I decided to write them a letter to tell them of my newfound, real relationship with Jesus and all the changes it had caused in me. I was sure they would be excited and relieved. In the letter I told what had happened in my life and what God had done for and in me. The letter concluded with, "While I still struggle with smoking once in a while and a few other remnants of my past, Jesus is the most important person in my life. I love Him and I know He loves me. I want to do whatever I can to further His kingdom."

The letter I received back from them started out businesslike. Cold. It proceeded to a blistering critique of my letter and the process of change I'd described. In conclusion, Hank and Lois voiced their doubts that I had become a Christian at all: If I'd really found the Lord, I wouldn't be struggling with so many things. How I could still smoke and call myself a Christian was beyond them. (This story is not about smoking, it's about accepting one another as believers. Please don't smoke. It will kill you. Not long after this incident, I quit.)

I experienced pain reading that letter. I was shocked by its intensity. I felt rejected and humiliated that I had trusted them as people with whom I could share my inner growth. I grieved the loss of friends I had assumed were on my side. I thought they cared about the real me. I was baffled that someone who had been through what they had could have so little understanding. And I felt profoundly sad at this realization—that Hank and Lois were more accepting of an unbeliever who hid his struggles than a believer who admitted them.

But what hurt the most was that I had been judged on the basis of my behaviors, not the reality of the inward transformation God had worked in me. The verdict? *Spiritually unacceptable!*

Lack of Acceptance

In Romans, Paul instructs believers to "accept one another, just as Christ also accepted us" (15:7). The Greek work translated "accept" is *proslambano*. It is a combination of words that mean *received toward yourself*, like drawing toward you something that belongs to you. In other places in Scripture, it's translated *admit to friendship*.

In contrast, the essence of judging is rejection. Judging is the opposite of acceptance.

In the kingdom of God, acceptance isn't based on whether you eat meat or don't eat meat (Romans 14). It's not based on whether or not you are circumcised (Galatians 6). Or if you smoke or don't smoke. In God's kingdom we are measured by the "new creation ruler." His acceptance, which is based on Christ's performance, is available in gift form to anyone who will accept it. (See Galatians

6:15–16.) Being judged hurts a lot because it communicates rejection.

Now in the early church, one group of Christians felt convicted about things like eating meat that had been offered to pagan idols. For them, apparently, it felt hypocritical to condemn the pagan religion but at the same time to benefit from it. Another group had no bad conscience about it, and quite possibly the poorer Christians felt blessed by this source of free meat!

Whose conscience was supposed to rule in this case? Whose *behavior* was right—the non-eaters or the eaters?

We find Paul's position in Romans 14:3–4:

> Let not him who eats regard with contempt him who does not eat, and let not him who does not eat judge him who eats, for God has accepted [*proslambano*] him. Who are you to judge the servant of another? To his own master he stands or falls; and stand he will, for the Lord is able to make him stand. [He continues in verse 13:]
> Therefore let us not judge one another anymore, but rather determine this—not to put an obstacle or a stumbling block in a brother's way.

In other words, Paul says, quit looking at the behavior of another believer and assessing him or her as unacceptable when God himself has accepted them. Instead, look at your own behavior and do the loving thing toward your fellow Christian.

This doesn't mean we are supposed to ignore outward behaviors or pretend we don't see wrongdoing. In fact, in 1 Corinthians 5, Paul tells us to judge the behaviors of those within the church. But notice the difference between this passage and the one in Romans 14. In 1 Corinthians 5, Paul is talking about the issues of immorality, coveting, swindling, reviling, drunkenness, and idolatry. These aren't gray areas, matters left to personal conscience or interpretation. We are to avoid those who call themselves Christians, yet do clearly immoral things because tolerating evil will have a leavening affect on those around, not because we are so spiritually superior we are beyond sinning ourselves. In this epistle Paul makes it clear that the gross offender is to be excluded from Christian fellowship while his fellow Christians attempt to bring him to his senses. The offender is to be dealt with in a way that brings repentance, release from sin, and then restoration to full fellowship. (See 1 Corinthians 5:3–5.)

Romans 14, on the other hand, is about self-righteous judging that results in "regarding your brother with contempt" (see verses 3 and 10). The word translated "contempt" means *to hold in less esteem*. This is about judging someone else to be spiritually inferior (and, of course, yourself superior) on the basis of what they do or don't do. So you can see that judging becomes hurtful when there is the element of spiritual superiority involved, or when expressions of personal faith or taste are treated as ultimate rights and wrongs.

Lack of Honor

I am a member of a world culture that treats me, by and large, as if what I do is significant and what I say has authority. Why? Because I am a male. The religious culture from which I came—for that matter, the one of which I am now a part—unfortunately seems to communicate the same message.

What is it like for a woman pastoring a small church in South Dakota to be called a "religious worker" by her denomination, instead of pastor, just because she's a woman? She does everything a pastor does. If a male was in her shoes he would be called a pastor.

Or how does it feel to have gifts and abilities, yet be restricted or prohibited altogether from exercising them based simply on anatomy? What must it feel like to be a Christian woman living in this world?

According to the letters I have received from Christian women who have been treated with lack of honor by the people of God, it feels like being *inferior* and *insignificant*. When they were little they didn't get picked for the team because they were *"just* girls." Now, it seems, they have been picked for the team—but they're "just women." (We'll look at this more closely in Chapter 7.)

As I said in Chapter 2, people need to know that they are special, that their lives have purpose. One of the ways they can experience this is in the treatment they receive from the people of God. "Be devoted to one another in brotherly love; give preference to one another in honor," Paul says in Romans 12:10. The Greek word translated "honor" is *time*, and means "give esteem of the highest degree." Literally, then, this verse says, "Cherish one another with a kindred affection, and outdo each other in esteeming the other to the highest degree." *Can you sense how terrific it would feel to be on the receiving end of this?*

The dynamic that erodes this experience, probably more than any other, is *favoritism*. Unlike judgmentalism, which is rooted in spiritual superiority, favoritism is simply about personal preference. It's based on a variety of factors we will examine.

The concept of favoritism is communicated in the New Testament with the Greek word *prosopoleptes*, "to show partiality." This concept is addressed many times in Scripture—for instance, in Romans 2:1, 1 Timothy 5:21, James 2:1, and others. We'll look at some of these shortly.

Probably the strongest statement about favoritism appears in James 2:8–9:

> If, however, you are fulfilling the royal law, according to the Scripture, "You shall love your neighbor as yourself," you are doing well. But if you show partiality, you are committing sin and are convicted by the law as transgressors.

James contrasts showing partiality against truly loving others. You don't do well to play favorites. You miss God's mark of how to act in relationships, because favoritism dishonors His people. Let's look at some examples of how the people of God play favorites and what God's Word says about it.

Showing Partiality

Partiality toward people with certain abilities or spiritual gifts.

How often have people been wounded because they were treated as if some spiritual gifts are better than others? Whole religious movements treat fellow believers like second-class citizens of the kingdom if, for example, they don't speak in tongues or prophesy. Other religious groups prefer members who don't "rely on emotional experiences."

For those of you who have experienced "charismatic" discrimination—in either direction—Paul has something to say to you in 1 Corinthians 12. He says that God has vouchsafed—on purpose and by design—a variety of people with a variety of gifts and ministries for the good of the whole (vv. 1–11). And not only has *God* conferred the gifts and ministries to people, He has even *placed* the people where He wants them throughout His body. Paul says that *every* person needs *every other* person (vv. 15–21).

For those of you who have felt as though what you do is unimportant, Paul reminds us that we are to bestow [clothe with] more honor on those who seem to be less significant. This isn't so that they will have *more* than the ones we naturally honor. It is so that there is unity and equal esteem for everyone in the body of Christ.

Let me tell you how I experience these principles. I am a writer and speaker—a public person. Because of that it seems easy for people to think that what I do is more significant than the behind-the-scenes person who backs me up. The truth is that if it weren't for that person and the gifted work she does that few people see, I couldn't do what I do. I would die a gruesome administrative death. And I'd look awful first.

Partiality toward those who haven't fallen into the "worst sins," and ill treatment of those who have.

Divorced believers have shared with me their feeling that they would have been treated better by Christians if they had murdered their spouse rather than divorced him/her—even those who have suffered terribly at the hands of a sociopathic and grossly abusive spouse.

The church has communicated through the ages—by a list of things that "cannot be talked about"—that there are some sins, some struggles, that are worse than others. Sexual sins and dysfunction fall into this category. I know a man who actually tried to castrate himself rather than ask for help from fellow believers for his sexual struggles.

Are some sins really worse than others? Not as far as God is concerned. Paul says, "For there is no partiality with God" (Romans 2:11). Peter tells us that God is the one who impartially judges according to each one's work (see 1 Peter 1:17). Every sin is equally serious. Outside of Christ, a person is condemned by any one transgression of God's law.

Yes, it's true that the ramifications that we and those around us may have to live with can be worse as a result of some sins. Our kids will be more hurt by our divorce than by our getting caught stealing a pack of chewing gum, for example. But don't you see? The fact that some problems have worse consequences only accentuates our need for the embrace and support of God's people. Instead, people have often experienced indictment and isolation from fellow believers who view some sins as worse than others.

And there is another area in which God shows no partiality:

> And opening his mouth, Peter said: "I most certainly understand now that God is not one to show partiality, but in every nation the man who fears Him and does what is right, is welcome to Him" (Acts 10:34).

God sees every sin and every sinner without favoritism. And He is also equally impartial in His response to repentant sinners, regardless of the nature of their sins. The psalmist reiterates this:

> For Thou, Lord, art good, and ready to forgive, and abundant in lovingkindness to all who call upon Thee (Psalm 86:5).

Partiality toward those who have or give large amounts of money.

In the town where I grew up, there was a wealthy family who basked in the respect of people in the community. One reason was that they owned a company that employed a large number of area people. This treatment carried over into their church. What they said was deemed weightier than the opinions of other people. The fact that they had money made them more important than everyone else.

There are churches that cloak the evil of it by adding a spiritual ingredient to the formula. They actually teach that having enough "faith" gets you God's favor. God's favor gets you money, too. Money proves your faith and gets you people's favor. Lacking money means you have somehow offended God or not found favor with Him.

This mind-set hurts people who struggle financially. Take Joanna, a believer who owns her own business. When Joanna's business took a downturn, she went through a time when she couldn't contribute as much to the church. The elders at her church confronted her for not giving. As a matter of fact, they said that her lack of giving was the reason her business took a bad turn.

Another believer from the same church, Jack, was an unscrupulous businessman. He cheated many of his customers, several of whom were also in the church. His actions were brought to the attention of the elders. But nothing was done or said because Jack was one of the main contributors to the church. Jack should have been confronted and his sin judged. Instead, he was honored.

Scripture blasts this kind of favoritism. Ephesians 6:9 tells us that when it comes to slaves and their masters, God shows no partiality. And look at what James 2:1–4, 6 says:

> My brethren, do not hold your faith in our glorious Lord Jesus Christ with an attitude of personal favoritism. For if a man comes into your assembly with a gold ring and dressed in fine clothes, and there also comes in a poor man in dirty clothes, and you pay special attention to the one who is wearing the fine clothes, and say, "You sit here in a good place," and you say to the poor man, "You stand over there, or sit down by my footstool," have you not made distinctions among yourselves, and become judges with evil motives? You have dishonored the poor man.

Partiality toward leaders.

First Timothy 5:17 says, "Let the elders who rule well be considered worthy of double honor, especially those who work hard at preaching and teaching." It's okay to esteem highly leaders who *rule well* and who *work hard at preaching and teaching.* If you notice you have leaders like this, find ways to show your appreciation.

But in some churches leaders are treated as though they are more special than other people *because they require it.* They get special discounts, special parking places, and special titles. In fact, Jesus says that there are leaders who love this *preferred treatment* (Mark 12:39–40). He tells believers to *beware* of this kind of leader, because they are the ones "who devour widows' houses."

In Matthew 23, Jesus cuts to the true heart of a spiritual leader. He says, "But the greatest among you shall be your servant" (v. 11). The Greek word for "servant" is *diakonos.* Forms of that word are found about one hundred times in the New Testament, and it means "table waiter." Another word, *doulos,* is used more than one hundred fifty times to describe how we are to conduct ourselves toward one another. This isn't a slave who has been caught and dragged off into captivity (like some poor pastors, who find themselves in the hands of demanding, controlling congregation members). This is a bondslave, someone who has *chosen* to sell himself into service.

In his book *The Jesus Style,*[1] Gayle Irwin says,

> Perhaps a good way to handle the trappings of leadership

---

[1] Proven Word Books, 1988, p. 58.

would be to put *Slave* over the doors of our plush offices and take away everything from the surroundings that is incompatible with that. You would not expect a slave to have a special parking space, more accessible than his master's. A slave would not have an office larger than others or more ornately decorated in order to show his position. A slave would not wear clothing that intimidated others or impressed them in any way except as being their servant. A slave would not try to use his "power" to protect his position of "first."

The problem of preferential treatment of leaders is at its ugliest when leaders are caught in sin. I know some leaders who have punished the people who try to hold them accountable. Others have sought special consideration for their sins—that is, asked people to ignore them—because they were leaders. This is clearly not the "double honor" Scripture commands—asking for God's people to be partial to leaders—and by overlooking sin, no less! I know some churches that have done this.

But Paul says,

> I solemnly charge you in the presence of God and of Christ Jesus and of His chosen angels, to maintain these principles without bias, doing nothing in a spirit of partiality (1 Timothy 5:21).

What principles is Paul talking about? Those he laid out in the preceding verses, which tell us how to hold leaders accountable. In fact, Paul is saying we are to hold leaders accountable *in a more public way than others* because they are leaders. And we are to make sure we show them no partiality because they are leaders.

It wouldn't be possible in this chapter to describe every circumstance in which God's people have suffered because of *favoritism*. But those of you who have experienced partiality in the body of Christ know the feelings of insignificance that accompany such ungodliness.

A man told me the hurt he experienced at the hands of an insecure church leader when he was rejected for being independent and outspoken in favor of another person who was passive.

Children in the body of Christ have been hurt because leaders' kids have received special treatment. Leaders' kids have been hurt because they have been held more accountable than other children.

People in the body of Christ are hurt as a result of partiality shown on the basis of height, weight, good looks, education, or lack of it.

The sad list goes on.

Showing partiality misses the mark.

Remember our basic inner needs: to know we are loved and accepted without strings; to know we are important, that we matter; to know we are not alone. Chapter 3 demonstrated that neglect pains us because it builds *aloneness*. And the two messages communicated through the dynamics of rejection, favoritism, and dishonesty described in the last two chapters are these: "You are not loved and accepted. And you don't matter." All three of these messages, dear friends, slanderously contradict everything God demonstrated when He chose to become one of us.

Many reasons prompt Christians to act in such hurtful ways toward one another, but one of the reasons is that leaders have led us down these unhealthy paths. That is why it's so important for leaders to be healthy. In the next chapter we will turn to the topic of what constitutes healthy—and unhealthy—spiritual leadership.

7

Let Down by Leaders

Earlier I promised that I would tell you more about Marie, the nineteen-year-old woman who wondered if I was a mandatory reporter. Here's the rest of her sad story.

Marie was wary of me for a long time. But after a few weeks I discovered the circumstances behind her question. While she no longer lived at home, her younger brother and sister still did, and they were being abused and neglected. Marie was experiencing extreme sadness and anxiety over their situation, angry that her parents would perpetrate such hurt on their own children. She was frustrated about her inability to help, and the weight of all these things had settled over her life in a fog of depression.

During that first session she had asked if I was a mandatory reporter so she would know what *not* to tell me. If I answered "yes," she would know that telling me about her brother's and sister's abuse meant I *should* report it to the state authorities. But that wasn't her past experience when she approached people in the church for help.

A year or so before, Marie had told her youth pastor about her own abuse. Ignoring the law regarding his duty to report abuse, he did not alert authorities—instead, she received a stern rebuke from the senior pastor for "not honoring her mother and father." So she told the school counselor, who did report. But the pastor, a good friend of her father, actually helped her parents stonewall an investigation!

It makes perfect sense why she didn't want to tell me what was going on. She had sought help from leaders in the church before, and they had let her down. She didn't want to be let down again.

Why Pick On Leaders?

I have chosen to spend an entire chapter on how Christians have been let down by Christian leaders for several reasons.

First, leaders *lead*. It's a sad-but-true fact that hurtful relationship dynamics often exist in churches because people imitate what they observe in their leaders. Instead of leading in the pursuit of truth, some leaders have led in engineering cover-ups or promulgating gossip.

This means, *second*, that leaders are more accountable for their behaviors and attitudes. It's a bigger deal when leaders are unhealthy and inappropriate. Why? Again, because people are following them. This is the reason, I believe, for Paul's teaching to Timothy:

> Do not receive an accusation against an elder except on the basis of two or three witnesses. Those who continue to sin, rebuke in the presence of all, so that the rest also may be fearful of sinning (1 Timothy 5:19–20).

In other words, much is at stake when a leader has been caught sinning. So Paul says to make certain the facts of the case have been corroborated before making a confrontation. But once the facts are clear, confront in the presence of all. This public attempt to resolve the problem will help people know they have been misled, so they can go in another direction.

Third, leaders are in a significant position to be able to use their authority to help people. When they fail at this—when they don't exercise authority in helpful ways—people are hurt and betrayed. Leaders mess up not only by *misusing* authority but by *neglecting* to use it when necessary.

Hence leaders—pastors, deacons, elders, teachers, anyone in the body of Christ followed by others—occupy a special accountability category all their own. Consequently, it matters very much how they lead. Notice the double-whammy involved. People are hurt when they are mistreated. But they are further let down when the leader, through example, has taught, validated, or led in the mistreatment by other believers.

In listening to wounded believers, through reading their letters and through my own observations, I have noticed that there are primarily two areas of abuse in which leaders let God's people down: not exercising authority, and giving improper spiritual direction. First, leaders have not exerted their authority for the purposes God intends. Second, many of God's people have been given spiritual direction that is irrelevant at best, errant and idolatrous at worst.

Authority

In Matthew 20, Jesus confronted a "Who's the Best Disciple Contest?" among His own followers.

You know that the rulers of the Gentiles lord it over them, and their great men exercise authority over them. It is not so among you, but whoever wishes to become great among you shall be your servant, and whoever wishes to be first among you shall be your slave (vv. 25–27).

The disciples certainly had an inimitable archetype of servant leadership in Jesus. At least one disciple finally understood what his master had said. Sometime later, Peter wrote:

Shepherd the flock of God among you . . . not for sordid gain, but with eagerness; nor yet as lording it over those allotted to your charge, but proving to be examples to the flock (1 Peter 5:2–3).

Misuse of Authority: *The Subtle Power of Spiritual Abuse* (Revisited)

It's important that leaders in the kingdom of God employ their authority to serve and protect God's people. Spiritual abuse results from the misuse of authority to boss, control, and overdirect.

Spiritual abuse is the mistreatment of a person who needs help, support, or greater spiritual empowerment, with the result of weakening, undermining, or decreasing that person's spiritual empowerment. Spiritual abuse occurs when a leader uses his or her spiritual position to dominate or control another person in the body of Christ.

It is not my intention at this point to reexamine every aspect of spiritual abuse or what happens to its victims. I would simply like to make the point that Christian leaders who use their authority to control do not accomplish the very thing for which they were given authority—to spiritually empower believers.

The apostle Paul says in Ephesians 4:11–12 that Jesus gifted apostles, prophets, evangelists, pastors, and teachers "for the equipping of the saints for the work of service [*diakonia*—to serve] to the building up of the body of Christ." Notice that Paul doesn't say that leaders were given to the church to *coerce, push*, or *goad* the saints for the work of service. He says we are here *to equip*.

How do we equip the saints to be servants?

Leaders help believers become servants by leading as servants, as Peter said, shepherding by "proving to be examples." That means being further ahead in serving than those following us.

Enabling

Leaders can compound their misuse of authority by what is called "enabling."

A word heard frequently in recovery and counseling circles, enabling means "equipping" or "making something possible." What I mean by enabling in relation to the misuse of authority is "unhelpful help, with good intentions." Let me illustrate.

I have known of many situations where a woman has sought help from her pastors because a problem her husband is having is destroying their home and marriage—even the husband himself. This might include substance abuse, workaholism, sexual addictions. Rather than addressing the real problem, though, the woman is told the reason her husband *has* a problem is that she is not "in submission." After all, if a woman is in full submission to her husband he won't have a problem with drugs, sex, greed, or alcohol— right? *This is incredibly destructive counsel.* And in the end, it enables the husband to stay sick and destructive.*

Failure to Use the Power of Authority

The people of God are also let down when authorities fail to use their powers to help. Pure passivity is what caused Marie's pain and disillusionment. Authority was *not* exercised when it should have been used to help.

This was also the case with Trudy, who wrote:

---

*I have gone to great lengths in my book *Good News for the Chemically Dependent*, Bethany House Publishers, to define and analyze this phenomenon. Refer to that work if you want to better understand enabling or the phenomenon of addiction.

I had a husband whose extreme work addiction led to our divorce on Tuesday of this week. He works for a Christian organization who rallied around him and even helped him with the details of the divorce. Not only was he not confronted, his workaholism was applauded by his superiors and he was heralded as a hero of the kingdom. Why don't these leaders understand the realities of work addiction?

After describing her own pain, Trudy talked about the hurt experienced by their son and daughter as a result of having an absentee father, compounded by their feelings of guilt for letting their "selfish" needs interfere with God's work. She ended the letter describing the addictive behavior patterns in their son.

Can you see what happened? Because the father's leaders did not lead him in a healthy direction, the son's leader—his father—took him in an unhealthy direction, too.

Adding Betrayal to Hurt

In family-of-God relationships, authority is meant to be exercised to restore the wounded, protect the vulnerable, and hold accountable those who abuse. But tragically this is often not how authority is used. Instead, the story goes like this: The abuse victim tells an authority about the abuse. The authority sides with the perpetrator and treats the victim like he or she was the problem for exposing the problem. Or they ignore the problem. As a result, there is no present-tense help for the victim. The offender isn't held accountable, so neither is there ongoing protection for the victim—or for other vulnerable people, for that matter. Wounds pile upon wounds.

Unfortunately, this scenario was what played out between Marie and her church family. She hoped her pastors would exert *some* kind of influence to stop the abuse in her family, even if it was just to call social services. Instead, she was made out to be the problem. Her church leaders did not use their authority to intervene. And God's little ones were left unprotected.

Perhaps one of the most epidemic examples of the "un-use" of authority in the church—and one of the most severely hurtful—is how sexual exploitation by members of the clergy has often been overlooked or hushed up. The perpetrator succeeds in the abuse and then succeeds in covering it up by manipulating a partnership of silence with the victim. How terrifying it is for the victim to shatter that power-hold by breaking silence and talking to another leader, someone in authority over the perpetrator. And how much more horrifying and hopeless it is to discover that the *leader's leader* is part of the conspiracy! First one leader misuses his authority, then other leaders lack the courage to use theirs.

No wonder victims are reluctant to come forward.

Yearning for the Church to Be Safe

A friend of mine is a counseling pastor in a church not far from Minneapolis. Several years ago he called and related an incident that had occurred in that church.

It had come to the attention of the pastoral staff that a man who was attending the church had been accused of sexually abusing children in several other churches. He had never been formally held accountable; he had just been more or less run out of town. A person in the singles' group also reported that this same man had tried to take indecent liberties with her at a singles' activity. And at the same time an unidentified woman called my friend to allege that this man had molested her eight-year-old daughter. She refused to identify herself and take the confrontation further, for fear her daughter would be re-victimized by the process.

Nevertheless, the leadership put her input in the pot with everything else they had heard and approached the man with their concerns. They also confronted him specifically with the behavior they had documented. While he did not deny the behavior, he actually denied that it was abusive! He was presented with several alternatives through which he could receive help. He rejected them all. He was told that it was necessary for him to receive help if he wanted to keep attending the church. He openly refused.

Then he asked the leaders, "What are you going to do if I keep coming anyway?"

They told him an announcement would be made to the congregation concerning his presence. The rationale was that people needed to make wise decisions concerning the safety of their children, and to do so they needed to have the correct information about the presence and problems of this man.

He then asked, "What if I come anyway?" To which they replied, "We'll call the police and have you arrested for trespassing."

He scoffed at their threat and left the meeting.

The next Sunday morning the pastor got up in front of the congregation and made the following announcement:

"*So-and-so* has been involved in behavior with children that is both immoral and illegal. He has refused to seek help. If you see him, know that he is under church discipline and not welcome here. You need to know this information so that you can make wise choices concerning your children in light of his possible presence."

Just as the pastor sat down—but before the choir director could get to the microphone—the man in question rushed up and made his own announcement:

"I'm the man the pastor just told you about. If you want to hear the true story about what's going on between me and leaders, come and see me after the service." At this point he was apprehended by four elders and carried out of the auditorium. The congregation parted like the Red Sea as they approached.

The man was physically restrained until the police arrived. One of the officers made it clear that if he didn't leave immediately, or if he returned, he would be arrested for trespassing. At that point he left and never returned.

That next week, telephones in the church office rang off the hook. Here is a sample of the calls that were received:

> We've been attending the church for almost six months. We've had a hard time deciding whether to stay or not. After what we saw on Sunday, we've decided that this is the church we want to be part of.
>
> I've never been part of a church where I've felt as safe as I do here. Thank you.
>
> It's so incredible to see a church where the small and vulnerable are actually protected and offenders held accountable.

God's people yearn for leaders to lead in a way that makes the church a safe place.

Rethinking 1 Corinthians 6

All of this has caused me to see 1 Corinthians 6:1–6 in a different light.

> Does any one of you, when he has a case against his neigh-

bor, dare to go to law before the unrighteous, and not before the saints?

Or do you not know that the saints will judge the world? And if the world is judged by you, are you not competent to constitute the smallest law courts?

Do you not know that we shall judge angels? How much more, matters of this life?

If then you have law courts dealing with matters of this life, do you appoint them as judges who are of no account in the church?

I say this to your shame. Is it so, that there is not among you one wise man who will be able to decide between his brethren, but brother goes to law with brother, and that before unbelievers?

I have always heard this text used to shame a Christian who was thinking of going to court against another believer, as if Christians are above legal accountability just because they are Christians. I do not believe that Paul is telling Christians not to press charges, not to hold other believers accountable when they have broken the law. In fact, God has instituted civil authorities to hold people accountable, Christian or not.

In reality, I believe Paul is confronting two issues here. Paul begins the text by asking, "How dare you . . ." with reference to going to the secular authorities. Why? It is not because someone is trying to hold a neighbor accountable. It's because the Corinthians were taking legal action because they underestimated the authority of the church. There is an authority even higher than the County Court Services—the body of Christ. That's the first issue Paul raises.

Secondly, Paul says,

I say this to your shame. Is it so, that there is not among you one wise man who will be able to decide between his brethren?

The sad implication is that the Corinthian church was evidently as impotent and irrelevant as the litigants had thought. As a result, they went outside the church to find justice. I believe that Paul's bigger issue is that the church was acting weak-kneed, not that someone had noticed the weakness and went somewhere else for help.

Direction

In the last section I made the point that it matters that leaders lead. Now I want to look more closely at the *manner* in which they are to lead.

First, as we've noted, leaders lead primarily by example. That's how Jesus led. He said, "For I gave you an example that you also should do as I did to you" (John 13:15). It's also how the Pharisees led. That's why Jesus told the people *not* to follow their example: "All that they tell you, do and observe, but do not do according to their deeds; for they say things, and do not do them" (Matthew 23:3).

Second, it matters immeasurably *where* leaders lead. The values, attitudes, and behaviors of any leader will affect the whole flock. As Jesus said: "A pupil is not above his teacher; but everyone, after he has been fully trained, will be like his teacher" (Luke 6:40).

I want to show you some of the unhealthy examples that have been set for the people of God.

Failing to Be Real

When I was in seminary a preaching professor told an entire class of people studying to be ministers, "Don't ever show people you struggle. Don't ever be vulnerable when you're in the pulpit. Don't ever show any neediness. People are looking at you to see how to live. You set the standard."

In effect, we were told not to be real. Now I don't believe pastors should make a practice of using the pulpit to solicit help and comfort from the congregation. But we were being taught to act like we were above the everyday pains and worries that are a normal part of human life—for the good of the everyday person in the pew, no less!

Is it any wonder there are so many churches where it's only OK to be OK?

That counsel is the spiritual equivalent of the pitch made on the deodorant commercial: "Never let 'em see you sweat." That's a fine tip if you're trying not to gross out your girlfriend or embarrass yourself in a job interview. But our Leader—Jesus—has shown us how to respond when faced with what life metes out. When His friend died, Jesus wept with the family. When the religious leaders did things in God's name that weren't glorifying God, He was angry and it showed. And in terror and agony about His impending torture, He sweat—"like drops of blood, falling down upon the ground."

Failing to Be Honest

As a young person in the ministry, one of the most common scenarios I faced were people coming to me about problems they had with others in the congregation. "I want to tell you what Bob did." Or, "Jane did such-and-such and I'm really hurt."

"Have you talked to them about it?" was my standard reply. People hated that answer.

"Well, no, I thought since you are the pastor I should talk to you."

"No," I would answer. "Since you have the concern or issue with them, you need to talk to them. It's not appropriate for you to talk to me if you haven't talked to them."

Sometimes they were intimidated by Jane or Bob. Then I would say, "If you want me to create a safe setting for you to share your concern with them, I'll do that. But you'll do all the talking."

When you have an issue with someone and you talk directly to them about it, that's called *having a relationship with them*. It's respectful. When you have an issue with someone and you talk to a third party about it—even if the content of the conversation is true—that's called *gossip*. Here's my point to other leaders: We are leading people to gossip when we allow them to talk to us instead of the person with whom they're having the problem. We are also enabling them to learn how to be dishonest and indirect in their relationships.

The stories I have heard of people wounded by gossip are innumerable. In almost every case the wounds were compounded by leaders who either took part in the gossip, or who, at least, didn't lead people to be honest in their relationships with each other.

The disillusionment of God's people is exacerbated when pastors stand in pulpits and preach that God loves the truth and hates lies, while they are dishonest in their relationships with people in the congregation.

Practical Irrelevance

It doesn't take a rocket scientist to notice when a church is irrelevant. This happens for a variety of reasons.

Sometimes meaningful causes get shelved because all of a church's energy and resources are being funneled toward things that don't matter. Or else things that matter a little get more attention than things that matter a lot. For instance, pastors and teachers in some churches are so preoccupied with end-times theology that the everyday needs of the people who are right under their noses are ignored.

Be honest. How much did you agonize this last week about the date of Christ's return—or whether it would be pre-tribulation, post-trib, or mid-trib? If you did, it was probably because it was a hot-agenda item for your leader. But I'll bet there are people reading this who wondered how their marriage would ever last, or where their teenager was at 3:00 A.M., or how they were going to pay the rent—and wondering where the church was when all this was happening.

It is true that the Old Testament prophets did proclaim an end to all time, when God wins and no one suffers. But even in the middle of this, they screamed at the top of their lungs for the people of God to quit neglecting widows, orphans, and other displaced people. And they railed against God's people for putting up with the evil political systems and hypocritical religious leaders of their day.

Nor does it take a rocket scientist to notice when a church is *boring*. I'm not saying it's the leader's job to keep people entertained, or that some important things in life aren't tedious. But in the heart of a human being is the need to know that his or her life matters, that it has a purpose. This was the hook in the *Four Spiritual Laws* booklet, a popular evangelism tool in the 1970s. "God loves you and has a wonderful plan for your life," it said. How people longed to know that they have a reason for being. And how people thronged to a God who could provide it!

Steven Curtis Chapman adroitly appealed to this heart's cry in his 1992 hit release, *The Great Adventure*. In it, he calls us to a life that's like "no other," a life that leaves sober-faced religion behind to do what we were created to do, explore new horizons. Chapman sings, "This is the greatest journey that the human heart will ever see!" God's love can lead us "far beyond our wildest dreams."

He's right!

When was the last time you thought of your life as a believer as a "great adventure"? The apostle Paul—concerned that the Galatians' sense of excitement had diminished—asked them, "Where then is that sense of blessing you once had?"

What "important" causes have you been led by your leaders to get excited about? *Are* they exciting? What have you been told truly matters? *Does* it really matter? To you, to other believers . . . to a world full of people who yearn for this life to matter? Really?

One more thing. We can watch a sports activity on television and get excited about the action and outcome. But it's not the same as being *in the game*. Admiring leaders or other believers as spiritual heroes is not the same as being a player yourself. Neither is wishing for the spiritual "good old days" of 20 or 200 or 2,000 years ago. Patriotic zeal isn't the same as spirituality, either. In fact, the United States is one of the few countries in the world where patriotism can masquerade as spirituality. And there are times when these things might actually distract from the "great adventure," the wonderful plan God does, in fact, have in store for our lives.

Idolatry

Finally, many believers have been lead into idolatry, a topic I will cover extensively in a later chapter. For now, I'll just make a short list of some of the gods we've been led to revere in order to meet our needs, to validate our worth, or to give us a sense of significance. Any of these things can take the place of God: church buildings, attendance figures, our own religious self-effort. And last but not least, many believers have had leaders who substituted *themselves* for God.

Consider these excerpts from a letter written by a disheartened couple in Indiana:

> In our church, a tremendous premium was placed on the "office of Pastor." No one was to call him by his first name, not even his wife. The reason we were given for this was that in order for us to receive blessing from the words he spoke we had to keep him in his office of Pastor. "When you call me by my first name alone, you cannot receive any blessing.
>
> "Some of you aren't hearing from God," our pastor would say. "See, God isn't going to speak to you without speaking the same thing first to your pastor." We're not just talking about scriptural interpretation here, this was also about personal matters. "There are people here with businesses, and you haven't told me what you're doing in them," he once preached. "There-

fore, your business is not covered, and it's not blessed because it does not have a pastoral covering. There's no anointing on what you are doing."

Some people finally left the church. Others who were belittled and shamed, those who decided to stay, would say to the pastor, "See how loyal I am to you. I knew there were Judases among us." They thrived on the acceptance of the pastor.

The Cry of a Leader

David, the shepherd of sheep, went on to become a great king, and probably one of the best loved of all the leaders of God's people. Despite his topsy-turvy tenure as king, he was a person who was called "a man after God's own heart." Let's hear that heart on the importance of healthy, relevant leadership as we bring this chapter to a close.

In Psalm 69:6 David says,

> May those who wait for Thee not be ashamed through me,
> O Lord God of hosts; may those who seek Thee not be dishon-
> ored through me, O God of Israel.

How different things might be for the people of God if this generation of leaders cared more about the honor of God than how to maintain a pastoral image or how to boost the number of people attending their churches!

Unprotected, bored, and led to depend upon puny caricatures of God—no wonder believers feel let down by their church and its leaders. Even by God.

Next we'll take a look at why this is so spiritually dangerous.

8

The Real Dangers

A number of years ago, our daughter Erin ordered her Christmas presents for the family from a mail-order catalog. She carefully picked out gifts for each one, lovingly matching them with the personality of each of her three sisters, her mom, and me. Then the wait was on.

When I told her that the long-awaited package had arrived, her face beamed. Her expression registered a little concern when she saw the size of the package, but she was off to her room to savor her acquisitions.

On Christmas, we were anxious to open these gifts that had given her so much joy to give. But Erin's excitement had diminished. In fact, she was acting embarrassed, even a little apologetic. Why?

The plaque for Mom that had looked so impressive in the catalog was less than a quarter of the size it appeared in the photograph. In fact, all the gifts were considerably smaller and more "delicate" than they appeared in the advertisement. Had she read the fine print she would have known this. But the deal was just too hard to pass up. So Erin was disappointed at how her surprise turned out. The products delivered by the company didn't meet up to the expectation created by the company's advertising.

Where Disappointment Comes From

Life is full of situations where reality doesn't live up to people's expectations. We expect to do really well on a test, but we get a C. We expect our boss to be excited with our just-completed project, but he or she barely acknowledges the effort. When reality comes short of our expectation, we feel disappointment. Disappointment is a common, normal part of life.

The degree of disappointment is usually determined by two factors: first, the degree of discrepancy between reality and our expectation—the larger the discrepancy, the bigger the disappointment; second, how important it is to us that our expectation be met. And so the more there is at stake, the bigger the disappointment when reality doesn't deliver.

The "Bait and Switch"

In the "Weird News" section of our weekly paper, I read of a man who ordered a mouse trap absolutely guaranteed to kill mice. He sent in his $5.99 and received a small box in the mail. In it he found two pieces of wood and a note. It read, "Place one board on a flat surface. Get the mouse you wish to kill to sit on the board. Strike it with the other board." No doubt the man was disappointed. But not as much as if the trap had cost him $59.99!

What I've just described is commonly called "bait and switch." A "bait and switch" is a tactic used by dishonest business people to sell next to worthless products. The "bait" is often the promise of easy prosperity, an "amazing" new product, or a deal that seems too good to be true. Once the customer goes for the bait, a "switch" takes place, and the customer—known as a "mark"—receives a fake, a substitute, or a product of such lesser quality that it's not at all what was promised.

Yet in all of the scenarios I just described, the *product* that arrived was not what created the problem. One time I ordered some "luxurious" duck-print bath towels that turned out to be more like big sheets of gauze. What if the advertisement for the towels had been honest: "Really cheap-looking, thin, scratchy towels—for only $12.99!" With a realistic expectation, this wouldn't have been a "bait and switch." If someone bought those towels, at least they would have done so knowingly, and when the towels came they wouldn't feel ripped off. The same holds true if Erin had paid for and expected 99-cent presents, or if the "mouse trap" had cost a dime and was advertised as a great gag-gift.

Honest ads, however, probably wouldn't have gotten the job done. Unscrupulous companies adept at creating a false expectation of reality are to blame. Their false advertising is the problem. Deceptive hearts and deceptive advertising teaming wits make something cheap look expensive. When I was in college I used to read a humor magazine. One of the regular features was called something like "This Is What You See—This Is What You Get." It showed how products, politicians, and corporations would really look if they were portrayed accurately.

What about in Christendom? *If* what believers actually experienced in the Christian life was advertised *accurately*, what would the cover of the bulletin—or the sign in front of the church building, or the advertisement in the Saturday paper—really say?

> Join us, and get more tired than you ever imagined.
> Be treated like a total stranger.
> Feel more guilt and shame than you have in any previous relationship.
> Experience new heights of boredom.
> Be discounted and excluded on the basis of gender.
> Agonize every day over whether your heavenly Father is pleased with you.
> Find that person you always wanted to have meddle in your personal affairs.
> Lose all hope of ever finding a healthy church.

If this is what's promised, people won't be so shocked when this is what they receive. But then, there won't be any takers either.

Some of you may feel offended at this use of satire to make a serious point. But is this list farfetched? Not according to the countless disheartened people I have seen in counseling. Not according to the letters we receive. And not according to the disappointed, disillusioned Christians who call every week. Why are so many Christians confused and in distress? It's because there is such gross discrepancy between what they experience and what they expected to experience *based on the advertising*.

What's at stake here is something of great importance.

Is God Guilty of False Advertising?

What does Scripture "advertise"—or represent to us—on behalf of God?

It's quite an impressive list. As we saw in Chapter 2, we have a welcome place in God's own family. A sense of belonging and support from our spiritual family members. Forgiveness for our mistakes, our bad choices, even our thoughts. Power on the inside to live victoriously on the outside. Rest from trying to find life from where life *isn't*. Freedom from having to perform to earn acceptance. The list goes on and on. And then, after all is said and done, we get to live forever in the presence of God who loves us.

If that's what you have actually experienced, you know why it's called the Good News—it's the best news! Have you experienced what you expected?

For many Christians, the answer is "no." For them, it feels like the Good News has been used as bait, then a kind of switch has taken place. But listen! In the case of the gospel, the problem is not with the advertising, or with the expectation it created. The problem is with the product-delivery system.

Somewhere along the line the delivery of our hoped-for product gets messed up. For example, David says, "[God's] anger is but for a moment, His favor is for a lifetime" (Psalm 30:5). Shouldn't God's people live in line with this principle God cares about? Is that an unrealistic expectation? Some Christians, however, have experienced favor for a moment—but that was only when they measured up to the expectations of other believers. The whole of their lifetime is spent dodging disapproval for minor offenses—some of which are not offenses at all, but matters of conscience.

Each one of us is "a letter of Christ," Paul says in 2 Corinthians 3:2. Jesus said, "Come to me, all who are weary and heavy laden and I will give you rest." He told His disciples, "A new commandment I give to you, that you love one another" (John 13:34). He said, "By this all men will know that you are My disciples, if you have love for one another" (John 13:35). Jesus has planned that there will be love among His followers. So it is not unreasonable for a Christian to come into a church and hope to find the extraordinary love of God there—love that has nothing to do with picayune fault-finding, love that is not self-centered, love that does not use a spiritual relationship for sick or carnal ends.

Yet for many people, as we have seen, relationships with other Christians have been the least accepting, most performance-based, most damaging relationships in their lives.

The apostle John says,

> And the Word became flesh, and dwelt among us, and we beheld His glory, glory as of the only begotten from the Father, full of grace and truth (John 1:14).

We are His body. It is not unreasonable for a Christian to expect to find grace and truth in the body of Christ. Yet many people have instead felt the sting of gossip, dishonesty, and abuse that would result in a lawsuit in any setting but the church.

The Worst "Bait and Switch" of All

Ask yourself these questions:

Can you imagine feeling so horribly tricked by a towel company that you would never again buy from *any* towel company? Is there any chance that you'd be so hurt or scared from the experience that you would avoid even *using* a towel? Actually, I received a "satisfaction guaranteed" clause with the purchase of my towels. If I had wanted to, I could have sent them back. Even if I couldn't have, the worst that could happen is that I'm out thirteen dollars, though a bit wiser and able to decide not to buy towels from that company again.

But a spiritual "bait and switch" is the ultimate worst-case scenario, from start to finish. And here's the real danger for you and me.

God, the one who faithfully keeps His promises, gets misrepresented by flesh-and-blood promise breakers. So people miss the true face of God because they see only the grotesque mask that's created by off-the-mark preaching and the misuse of His Word and His name. The kind intent of His will gets perverted by the human fine print. The heirs miss out on enjoying their divine inheritance because they got stuck with a counterfeit. The danger is compounded when you're not allowed to notice the fake.

People go in the opposite direction from God because He receives the blame for all this.

Christians who have been baited with the glories of the kingdom of God are then trained, or tricked, into settling for a caricature of their spiritual inheritance. Some of God's sons and daughters are so let down they're afraid of relationships with other believers. Others grow confused, nervous, or skeptical about God.

Recently I got a letter from a woman whose pastor told her that God loved her and wanted her to be His child. As she had grown up in an abusive family and had never experienced acceptance, this was music to her ears. She bowed her knees, right there in his office, and gratefully entered into a saving relationship with that God. The pastor then said that now that she had given her heart to God, she would be better off if he just shot her dead. He said that if she lived another day she would fail God and lose her salvation. Do you see the bait and switch? Fortunately, she spotted it, and she didn't blame God for the pastor's evil maneuver. Nevertheless, she was extremely confused by the event, and a chasm of distrust had opened up between her and other Christians.

What's ironic about this is that the pastor no doubt had good intentions when he did this. More than likely his goal in the comment was to spur her on to a better lifestyle than she had lived in the past. Whatever his motive, what he said was a misrepresentation of God and the freeing gospel of salvation by grace. And his maneuvering drove a wedge between a new Christian and the body of Christ.

A Night at the Restaurant

Just the other night Holly and I were at a restaurant. Originally we hadn't intended to order dessert. But right there, wedged between the salt and pepper shakers, there was a beautiful, full-color dessert menu. On the cover was a picture of a piece of peach pie, brimming with slices of fresh peaches smothering a layer of cheesecake filling. You know the rest of the story. When our piece of pie came, it looked nothing like the picture at all. Our bogus piece had one measly peach slice, and it was dried up at that. *What a rip-off.*

Whether or not the folks at the restaurant intended to mislead us is not the issue. We *had* been misled, and felt a bit cheated. Did they think we wouldn't notice? We felt embarrassed, even selfish at the prospect of calling it to our waiter's attention.

When it was time for me to pay up, I said to the waiter, "We didn't eat our dessert and I don't believe I should have to pay for it. It wasn't anything like what was advertised." In a respectful, even apologetic voice he replied, "No problem, I'll deduct the price from your bill. Thank you for telling me." This man would rather have me tell him about a problem so he could correct it than have me leave and never come back.

I didn't tell that story to suggest that we should be nit-picky whiners threatening to leave every time we don't get exactly what we want at church. Sometimes we have to accept the fact that we aren't going to have everything our way. That's okay in the body of Christ when we're talking about things that don't have eternal consequences and don't damage our relationship with God. I told the story as an example of someone who took responsibility for not delivering what was promised. A restaurant exists for the purpose of making money. And the waiter, a total stranger, treated me with respect and not as if I was the problem for pointing out the problem.

As we have seen in the previous chapters, when people come into God's family it is with raised hopes and expectations. No, imperfect human beings will not always be able to deliver in full what is described. (Please read that last sentence again.) *This is the nature of people and relationships.* But in too many churches people do not experience a response as gracious as the waiter's. It seems they're expected to keep quiet and settle for something bogus. Some have even found it easier to leave and never come back than to be criticized, blamed, and ostracized for talking about a discrepancy so that it can be corrected.

A Lot at Stake

It is dangerous to misrepresent God. The promises made to believers in the New Testament are not some kind of spiritual dessert. They are the spiritual main course. We're talking about learning how the support of other believers can help us live as citizens of a kingdom we cannot touch, as sons and daughters of a Father we cannot see. How we can live in a way that confronts and changes the world around us. How, with God's help, we can take back lives and families that have been held captive by the evil one. We have joined up with an army that is storming the gates of hell!

And in God's family we are better than customers. *We are sons and daughters of God.* We are fellow-heirs and fellow-servants of God with the other members of God's family.

Though the emphasis of this book is on healing, it's okay to spend the time you need focusing on the hurts you've received—especially if no one has given you permission to do so before. And it's also okay to hold each other accountable to be the body of Christ.

When the time comes, you will need to reenter the race you were running before the wounds and neglect of fellow believers sidelined you. As we saw in the opening chapters, you and I were created to be vessels of the Holy Spirit of God. And there are forces at work against us. Sometimes it's hard to distinguish the work of our Adversary from the damage that's caused by those in our own family. It feels as if the "wolf" has infiltrated the flock and bitten us pretty hard.

The aim of this first section of the book was to help you understand the nature of your wound and to help you make the distinction between God's faithfulness and the failings of His family. Though God's family may have let you down, God himself is true, and His promise of a safe place of inward rest, growth, and support is still good. It is *solid*.

Now, in the second section, we'll look at how you get back in the race . . . and win.

Part Two

Introduction

For some of you reading this book, the destructive nature of your past contact with other Christians has driven you to isolate yourself—physically or spiritually—from others in the family of God. Furthermore, your pain is threatening to keep you out of the "race" altogether. Yet it doesn't have to end this way, with you protecting a wounded hope in isolation. Don't let it!

There is a way back into a relationship with God and full fellowship with members of His family that is healthy and safe. It's going to take something on your part to rebuild the bridge of trust. You may have to fight your way back. While you aren't responsible for the wounds, you can and must take responsibility for your recovery from them. In the end, it will not matter so much what's happened to us or how we were treated. What will tell the tale of our lives is how we responded to those things and how we grew stronger in the image of Christ because of them.

Maybe you are too disillusioned or spiritually exhausted to fight right now. Consider this letter from someone who is in that condition:

> I would like to offer my appreciation for your book, *The Subtle Power of Spiritual Abuse*. I would like to encourage you to continue the good work by publishing a sequel. There seems to be a lot more to be said.
>
> Mostly, I would really like to know how a church that truly practices grace should work. After being in the church my whole life, all I have seen is sheep abusing the shepherd, or shepherds abusing the sheep. I can't even begin to comprehend anything else. The only viable solution I've come up with is to get out of the system and stay out. It seems beyond re-

demption to me. There's no such thing as the church as far as I can tell. I'd like to be proven wrong, because I'm rather like a refugee or an exile. I have no "country" as it were. And that leaves me somewhat without purpose.

If this is also your story, *rest*. Find one friend you can trust, then take a look at yourself and your wounds. In the grace of God, you have all the time you need. Or perhaps you are too hurt or stuck to begin your comeback on your own. If this is the case, seek out a competent, qualified professional counselor to help you begin a process of healing. Remember, "where two or three are gathered together, there I [Jesus] am also."

I offer the following chapters as a resource of support and encouragement as you find your way back into an active and meaningful life with Christ and with other Christians.

Here are some of the questions I will seek to answer along the way:

What will happen if I try one more time?
Are there things I have done, or things I'm doing now,
    that contribute to my being stuck?
How can I avoid another hurtful situation—
    or deal with it in strength if it happens again?
How do I overcome the depression I experience?
Will I ever be able to trust again?
Is there such a thing as a healthy church?

Beyond your own efforts, you will also discover a greater healing power at work. God is a God of redemption. He has a history of turning apparent defeats into victories. He loves to rescue lost situations, relationships, and people. Your story does not end with the hurts caused by the unfortunate, even evil ways people act in His name. What was meant for evil can be turned into good. As your wounds turn into new strengths, let's see what He will do.

9

Why Does This Happen?

Not long ago I received a letter from a couple in Nebraska. They told me they had heard that I was counseling a good Christian friend of theirs, named Corrie. They were happy she was finally seeing someone for her many problems, which they said they had noticed through their friendship with her. They went on to say that while they had never voiced their concerns to Corrie personally, they'd like to share their numerous observations with me. They wanted me to be aware of Corrie's issues so I could "do a better job of ministering to her." Then came this statement: "By the way, please don't tell Corrie that we wrote or that you got any of this information from us."

I didn't ever finish the letter. When I read that last statement I folded it up and sent it back. Why?

First, I had no way of knowing if what this couple was saying was true. Perhaps it was. But under the circumstances, for me to act on it would have been disrespectful of Corrie and could have caused great harm. It would also have been enabling the couple *not* to have their own relationship with Corrie. Besides, if they weren't willing to take personal responsibility for their concerns for Corrie, why did they think I would be willing to address them secondhand?

As far as I'm concerned this couple was gossiping. This was a far cry from Paul's instructions: "Laying aside falsehood, speak truth, each one of you, with his neighbor, for we are members of one another" (Ephesians 4:25). They were functioning as if the Bible really said, "When you have a problem with someone, *triangle* someone else into the picture to do your relational work for you instead of talking to the person." Their reluctance to communicate honestly with Corrie herself—and their efforts to use me to fix her—told me the true nature of their "friendship." It also told me that as long as they came across *looking* nice, sweet, agreeable, and positive to others, that's what really counted in their book. They would never have to risk upsetting anyone that way. Because surely upsetting someone in any way would make them feel like the bad guys, and who likes to feel bad?

This is self-idolatry.

Well-Intentioned but *Hurtful* Help

There's no question that this "triangling" behavior happens throughout the church. And if you've ever been on the receiving end of it—unintentional or not—you know how hurtful it can be. You feel exposed and betrayed if the information is true, discounted and framed if it isn't. The question really is: Why do Christians act this way toward one another?

If you were to pose that question to the couple in Nebraska, I'm sure their answer would be, "We wanted to help—our intention wasn't to tear down but to build up." While not everyone is so well-meaning, let's give these folks the benefit of the doubt. Let's say their intentions were honorable. So why would someone whose intentions are to help and strengthen act in a way that could produce results exactly opposite of what they hoped for? Furthermore, why would Christians act in a way that contradicts the *teaching* of Scripture when they no doubt would defend its *authority*? If you asked these people if it is okay to act in ways that contradict the Bible's instructions—just because we are well-intentioned—they would answer with a resounding "No!" But well-intentioned gossip is still gossip. It still misses God's mark for acting in a way that builds healthy relationships. So we're back to the question—Why do we act this way?

At the risk of sounding simplistic, I believe the answer is this: People do what they have learned. My strong suspicion is that the couple from Nebraska attempted to triangle me into their relationship with Corrie because that's what they knew to do. They had never gone to Corrie with their honest observations because that isn't what they had seen done by others. It's likely that no one in their circle of family and friends had provided correction for this behavior so they could learn a more healthy one.

I'm not using the word "learned" in the sense of "receiving the right information," because I'm guessing they had read their Bibles. If you tested them on whether they knew the right information, they would pass the test. And along with their intentions, we'll give them the benefit of the doubt that they sincerely want to obey what they know of the Bible.

Rather, I'm using "learned" the way Paul uses it in Philippians when he says, "I have learned to be content," (4:11), and "I have learned the secret" (4:12). The first "learned" is translated from the Greek work *emathon*. It is from the same root word from which comes the Greek word *mathatais*, which means "disciple." Both of the processes of being discipled and being initiated involve experience and practice. Paul was discipled or taught, and Paul was initiated by experience, and so he was brought to a state of having learned.

Learning Unhealthy Relationship Skills

Each one of us is in the "state of having learned." We learned not to drive through a red light, not to yell "fire" in a crowded theater, and not to make jokes about weapons while going through the checkpoint at the airport. These kinds of lessons are learned through experience, either ours or someone else's. In addition, we learned to tie our shoes, use a spoon, brush our teeth, and drive a car. Learning these skills involved practice. In both cases, people have taught us these things, either by imparting information or by providing opportunities to practice, or both.

Our past relationships with people have informed, discipled, and initiated us into the way we now live, including the way we conduct ourselves in relationships—even those with other members of God's family. For many of us, though, our past relationships failed on two vital counts. First, they didn't teach us (disciple or initiate through practice and example) to act in ways that were healthy and beneficial to relationships. This can be true even if the information we received was correct. Second, they taught us (discipled or initiated through practice and example) to act in ways that were hurtful to relationships. This can happen even if the actions contradicted the teaching. Ironically, we humans have a tremendous capacity for saying and teaching and *believing* one thing, and doing another, never noticing the discrepancy. This is blindness, one reason we need each other. Ironically, too, bad behavior is often modeled with good intentions.

Let me illustrate with an example from our family. Let's say one of my daughters comes to me and says, "*So-and-so* (a sister) has taken my marking pencils!" She's telling me because I'm a powerful person in the family and she wants me to fix the situation. My goal as a parent is to empower this daughter to do her own relational work in order to resolve the situation and restore the relationship. When she's twenty years old and I'm not around, she will need to know how to do this kind of thing, regarding issues a whole lot bigger than purloined pencils.

So I reply, "Have you talked to your sister?" She may answer "No." I then say, "You need to talk to your sister. Tell her how you feel and what you want." If she does this and gets her markers back, the situation is over and a relationship is restored. But she might be afraid to talk to her sister. She's small and her sister is big. So then I would offer to go with her to lend her some of my authority by my presence. But she is still going to have to do the talking, which she is now able to do as a result of being empowered by me.

If instead I simply take the mooched markers away from her sister, I have accomplished, in my estimation, several undesirable goals. First, I've taught daughter number one that if she has a problem with someone, there's a quick payoff, and easy solution, in talking to a third party instead of the person with whom she has a problem. Second, I have enabled my two daughters to avoid having their own relationship. And third, I have *not* discipled or initiated my daughter in a relationship skill that will benefit her and her relationships in the future. How could I expect something different in their later, adult relationships if they learned these bent relationship habits as a child?

Passing On a Relational Legacy

I chose the above example from my family rather than from church life because families provide the primary relationship context in which people are informed and discipled in how to have relationships. The relational seeds—of ways we act in relationships—are so deeply planted there that they bear fruit in future generations of relationships. That's why it is so important for our families to be healthy. And it's also why, like noxious weeds, unhealthy relationship skills sprout again throughout our lives. For good or for bad, from childhood on we carry a legacy of relationship skills into our adult relationships.

In the book *Tired of Trying to Measure Up*, I discussed ten dynamics that characterize unhealthy families. At this point I want to recall those characteristics and describe the skills that people learn—or fail to learn—in order to survive those family systems. I think this information will help you understand how it is that people in their new family, the church, often act in such unhealthy and hurtful ways. In many cases they are simply doing what they learned.

The following is a list of the traits of unhealthy families. I include descriptions of their *dynamics*, their *effects* upon family members, and ways these effects are *recycled in church relationships* at a future date.

1. *Shaming messages*

Dynamics: Communicating to people in overt ways that they are unacceptable, inadequate and worthless—that something is wrong with them.

Effects: Members can become accustomed to being put down. Some people actually "need" to feel guilty and indicted before they can put forth more positive effort. Feeling bad enough becomes the power that motivates them to do good. People learn a vocabulary of self-indictment and condemnation of others.

Recycled in the church as:

- Sermons that constantly remind God's precious sons and daughters about *who they used to be* instead of *who they are now*.
- Name-calling, comparing, and shaming our kids in Sunday school classes.
- Mistaking berating and condemning for exhorting.
- Confusing self-degradation with true humility.

2. *Performance-orientation*

Dynamics: Human beings flourish in environments where love and acceptance are gifts, bestowed because of who we are. But performance-oriented relationships do not convey this much-needed, unconditional love. Instead, value and acceptance are earned on the basis of performance. Acceptable performance also becomes the main way to protect against being treated in hurtful ways. Performance always seems to fall short, however. In the end, what's reinforced is the message of defectiveness and lack of acceptability.

Effects: Family members try desperately to live up to the standard, or else they learn that nothing measures up and give up in despair. People's self-assessment goes up and down like the stock market, based upon what they do and upon what people think about what they do.

Recycled in the church as:

- Christian "formula seminars," books and sermons designed to produce everything from holy living to God's perfect plan for your garden.
- Legalism, or assessing and earning God's acceptance based on doing or not doing certain behaviors.
- Self-righteousness or, in more practical terms, a positive self-assessment derived from performance of Christian lists—including traditions, cultural customs, and even the personal preferences of others.
- Shame and self-condemnation for failure to measure up to the pressure of the religious crowd that claims to speak for God.
- Judgmentalism, as members of God's family assess themselves spiritually acceptable compared to each other.
- A kind of spiritual competitiveness between believers.
- Confusing obsessive religious behaviors with dedication.
- Confusing pretending with submission.

3.Government by unspoken rules

Dynamics: Rules that reign supreme in unhealthy families are seldom spoken out loud. The reason? When said out loud the rules tend to sound as unhealthy or unreasonable as they actually are. (For instance, "How things look is more important than what is real." Or, "Adults are more important than children.") You discover that one of these rules exists only when you question or break it. These rules have more power than the ones we say are important, the ones we say out loud. (For instance, "Being nice is more important than being honest" has more influence over people's behavior than "Speak truth each one of you with his neighbor.")

The most powerful and damaging of all the unspoken rules is the "can't-talk" rule. This rule keeps the truth quiet because talking about a problem—admitting it exists—is the problem. You're the problem for saying there's a problem.

Effects: Family members learn to live by rules with which they would disagree if heard out loud. People learn to "protect" closeness with others that doesn't even really exist—a false unity—by keeping the truth from each other. Unspoken rules create double standards between the rule-makers and the rule-followers. This leads to lack of accountability on the part of the rule-makers, and confusion, fear, anger, and resentment on the part of the followers.

Recycled in the church as:

- Rigid leadership that cannot be held accountable. Noticing or questioning inconsistencies and attempting to bring accountability results in punishment.
- A "choker chain" style leadership or management. God's people are afraid to exercise their freedom in Christ since it is never clear when the chain of authority will get yanked. Because lip-service is paid to freedom and respect, this is also very hard to confront.
- Much effort on the part of members to get "next to" leadership. Once again, "closeness" is based on performance, pretending to agree, not noticing incongruities between teaching and lifestyle, and loyalty to a leader in the face of the concerns of those who do notice.
- Confusion, frustration, and resentment on the part of God's family members, and guilt and shame for feeling these things.
- Things said in private that people won't admit in public.
- Confusing "peace at all costs" with true peace.

4. *Speaking in codes*

Dynamics: Saying things honestly, openly, and directly makes you the problem, so you learn to talk in codes.

Effects: Family members develop great "radar," or the ability to pick up tension in situations and relationships. People learn to say things in code instead of saying them straight. They also learn to decode what other people aren't saying straight. This is necessary in order to stay out of trouble.

Recycled in the church as:

- Learning how to hint or manipulate to get what you need without directly asking, because needs are "selfish."
- Speaking as if you are representing the needs and concerns of others rather than your own.
- Gossip—talking about people instead of to them.
- Confusing saying things crookedly or not at all with speaking the truth in love.

5. *Idolatry*

Dynamics: Any time we rely upon *resources* to meet our needs instead of God who is the *Source*, it is idolatry. Some of the idols in unhealthy families are: the opinions of others, appearance, mood-altering substances, religion, performance of the children, the spouse's performance, things. Instead of people and things being treated as gifts—resources from the one true Source—they are treated as if they have power to validate those who depend upon them.

Effects: Jean Antonello, author of *The Anti-Diet Book*, says that people from these kinds of families become "OPIOOM" addicts (Other People's Inferred Opinions Of Me). They are dependent upon what other people think for their sense of well-being. What is real, true, and honest gets lost in the service of image. Things become more important than people.

Recycled in the church as:

- Pouring money into buildings instead of people.
- Continuing to expend energy, time, and resources on activities that meet no real needs, because "we've always done things this way."
- Peace and unity sacrificed in service to, for instance, the color of the hymnals or the right Bible translation.
- Confusing our will to do God's will with God's will.

More on idolatry in the next chapter.

6. *Having a hard time with the kids*

Dynamics: Normal kids are in the trial and error process of learning how to live—but they haven't gotten there yet. But in this way of thinking everything is riding on their flawless conformity to rules. What other adults in this system think of parents is based upon their children's behavior. Consequently, trying isn't good enough, and errors are forbidden—or if they can't be forbidden they are covered up.

Effects: Children learn to act like miniature adults. Having fun and being spontaneous is too risky, so kids learn to be somber and serious. People can't take a joke. They also learn that the weight of their parents' well-being is resting on their performance. Consequently, they either perform well to carry that weight, or they rebel to throw it off.

Recycled in the church as:

- The mood of the leader determines the members' sense of well-being.
- People act overresponsible, thus enabling others to be under-responsible, both of which are equally irresponsible.
- Confusing someone's overresponsibility with leadership.
- Somber, overcontrolled Sunday school classes.
- People feel like they are responsible to control God's "mood

swings" and reactions with their behavior.

- Adults tend to feel that if there is a problem they must have caused it, or they're supposed to fix it.
- Mistaking quiet, fearful compliance for respect.

7. *Fault and blame*

Dynamics: Once again—because people are accepted on the basis of behaviors—finding fault and assigning blame serves the purpose of assuring that it is you, not me, that is credited with the mistake. The guilty party must be found so that they can be exposed and humiliated sufficiently to prevent similar behaviors in the future. This is not the same as holding people accountable for their behaviors and helping them take responsibility for their actions, both of which empower people to be healthy.

Effects: People are reluctant to admit wrong choices, or even mistakes, because of the shame and humiliation they receive. Lying becomes less painful than telling the truth. Ways must be found to avoid taking responsibility. People become strong on "head" skills.

Recycled in the church as:

- People who have a hard time taking responsibility for their choices.
- Others who spend a lot of energy trying to make them.
- People who have a hard time with gifts—grace, forgiveness, acceptance all seem too easy.
- Christian service to alleviate guilt or because we are so undeserving and we owe God so much, instead of because we love Him and His people.
- An understanding that behavior can't initially gain God's approval (saved by grace through faith), yet living as if spiritual growth from that point on depends on personal effort. (In other words, "white knuckle" the Christian life—and if you pull it off, call it "God.")
- Confusing punishment (making people pay) with discipline (helping people learn).

8. *Strong on "head" skills*

Dynamics: Because every word and every action has the power to indict and demean, people use their heads to rationalize, debate, minimize, and justify. Questions are used to trap, not teach.

Effects: Again, people learn ways to shift responsibility from themselves onto anything or anyone else. Rationalizing is taken to an art form.

Recycled in the church as:
- Exceptions to the rule that apply to one group of people but not another.
- Being clear of your question or confrontation of people ahead of time, absolutely confused and feeling crazy afterward.
- Taking Scripture out of context to justify actions.
- Confusing a person's ability with their "anointed" words.

9. *Weak on "heart" skills*

Dynamics: The fact that someone feels hurt may mean that a person—not merely circumstances, or a system—is doing the hurting. But responsibility is never taken, blame is always found. The person hurt becomes the problem for being oversensitive, instead of the "hurter" being responsible for the hurting. Feelings are wrong, needs are selfish.

Effects: People don't learn a language to express feelings because they pretend not to feel what they really do feel. In an effort to escape feelings, people are controlled by them. They also pretend not to need what they really need.

Recycled in the church as:
- Feelings are discounted or condemned.
- Instead of just saying, "I feel hurt, I need help," people put on fake smiles and quote cliches and Bible verses to deny feelings. Feeling pain isn't "victorious."
- Instead of giving comfort, the church offers liturgies of cliches and Bible verses to condemn or fix people who express their feelings.
- Meeting everyone else's needs (which evidently are okay) at the expense of asking for help yourself. After all, needed help is unspiritual, needs are selfish.
- Confusing martyring your own needs with showing mercy.
- Confusing pretending not to have pain with joy.
- Confusing the pretense that you have no struggles with victory.

10. *Full-looking empty people.*

Dynamics: Since love and acceptance have to be earned with performance, people learn to act in ways that are appropriate and acceptable. But only unconditional love and acceptance truly meet our deepest needs. Conditional love disappoints and exhausts. Hence, people may look full on the outside, while they are empty on the inside.

Effects: People learn to respond to external pressure to perform. What is real on the inside is ignored or lost completely. Therefore, because "safety" comes from the outside and not from the inside, barriers are erected for protection, including rules: controlling what people wear, read, and listen to; keeping them away from certain people; sending them to (certain) Christian schools. How things look is more important than what is real. Giving the right answer is more important than giving the true one. It is more important, for instance, that people *think* you have a good marriage, than that you really have one.

Recycled in the church as:

- Hypocrisy
- Thinking that the world will get a good impression of God from how well Christians pretend they don't have problems.
- Placing on a pedestal those believers who are able to maintain outward appearances.
- Ignoring or rejecting those who are more characteristic of the ones to whom Jesus ministered—that is, those whose problems and pain on the inside seep to the outside.
- Confusing looking healthy with being healthy.
- Confusing faithful (regular, habitual) giving and church attendance with faithfulness.

Can you now better understand where problems come from? It's no surprise that the relational skills learned in families characterized by the traits above carry over into church life. Contrary to the healing, building, teaching, and encouraging that occurs in God's family when the "one anothers" characterize our relationships, we see God's people being hurt and let down. And their pasts are repressed or repeated "in Jesus' name," instead of being redeemed by His power and truth.

While it is true that we have been hurt, we *will* choose, and we *are* choosing, how to respond.

Will we triumph or remain victims? The *American Heritage Dictionary* defines a victim as: *1. One who is harmed or killed, as by accident or disease. 2. One who is tricked, swindled or injured.*[1]

Are there believers who have been harmed, tricked, swindled or injured, on purpose or by accident, in their relationships with other members of God's family? There is no doubt. But we can, we *must*, move on into victory—not only in our personal relationship

---

[1]*The American Heritage Dictionary* (Dell Publishing Company, New York: copyright 1983), p. 757.

with God, but even in our relationships with His people.

In Chapter 10 we continue on our road through recovery by addressing the first step we need to take to progress from victim to victor.

10

From Victim to Victor

This last spring I had the opportunity to present a workshop on spiritual abuse to a group of people in Toronto, Canada. The group was actually made up of three groups of people who had been deeply hurt in three very different church settings. In fact, had it not been for the common denominator of spiritual abuse, under normal circumstances these people might not have even talked to each other. They were that diverse—but here they were. They had found and clung to one another, trying desperately to make sense of their experiences and move on to reenter the life of Christ in relation to the church.

I had spent the first evening defining spiritual abuse and describing the characteristics of spiritually abusive churches. The next morning I described the wounds and struggles common to people who have abused in these places. Then I began the afternoon session by outlining some of the issues that were important in the process of healing. About twenty minutes into the presentation a man raised his hand—I thought, to ask a question. When I called on him he pointed out the window to some tangled brush across the driveway and said, "See that mess over there? The leadership of our churches led us into a spiritual tangle of confusion that was like that mess, and they shouldn't have. It was wrong of them to do it. But do you know what? *We followed.*"

What an important insight. Someone led, but I followed. Someone acted, but I responded. Someone was responsible for what they did. But I am responsible for what I did.

There is incredible freedom and power in the words I AM RESPONSIBLE.

What Am I Responsible For?

"What can *you* do differently?" I probably ask my counselees this question—or one like it—more than any other. A wife comes in and tells me countless stories of her husband's irresponsible behaviors. "What can *you* do differently?" Parents come in with a grocery list of ways their teenager's out-of-control escapades are throwing the entire family into a turmoil. "What part of the turmoil are *you* responsible for?"

I am not asking the question to imply that the wife or parents are responsible for *causing* their loved one's actions. I'm not implying that if they change, their loved one will automatically change. Actually, their loved one might never change—he or she has that choice. What my question points to is the fact that while people can't control their loved one's choices, they can make free choices of their own.

This is what the man in Toronto realized. Somewhere in the presentation he asked himself the question, "What am I responsible for?" It provided him with a starting point on the road to his healing. His answer—"I followed"—was the first milestone he passed that told me he was going in the right direction.

While it is a liberating question—one with which everyone who seeks health must come to grips—it's a question that must be asked at the proper time. Asking the question before there is some understanding and healing can cause more hurt. And it can be interpreted not as empowering but as blaming the victim—that is, that the abuse was your fault.

Understanding Blame Vs. Holding Accountable

We need to grasp this important idea. One of the concepts that must be understood so the question can be empowering is this: There is a difference between blaming others and holding them accountable. For instance, let's say five-year-old Rick is beaten by his dad. What does Scripture say (besides that dads shouldn't beat their kids)? It says that he should talk to his dad. But he's learned that whenever he tries to talk to his dad about how he's been treated (to hold the dad accountable for his behavior) he gets hurt again—sometimes even worse than the first time. His dad notices Rick shutting him out with a surly disposition. "What's going on with you?" asks the dad. To protect himself from further hurt Rick chooses to pretend that nothing is wrong. He pastes a fake smile on his face and then he chooses to lie. "Nothing. I'm okay."

Who is responsible for what? The dad is responsible for the abusive behavior. He is also responsible for his reactions to Rick's confrontations in the past that have communicated to Rick, "If you try to hold me accountable for my actions, I will hurt you again." Is the dad accountable—that is, should his actions be charged to his account? Yes. If I had been involved I would have called the county child protection services, someone bigger than the dad, to hold him accountable.

But Rick is accountable for the pretending and lying. Does it make sense that Rick chose these actions? Yes. In fact, with the power differential that exists between Rick and his dad, it could even be argued that Rick really didn't have any choice but to lie. But the truth is, he did. So he chose to protect himself by lying, rather than choosing to tell the truth and risk being hurt again. In fact, it might have even been a "wise" choice under the circumstances. A five-year-old cannot protect himself by filing a restraining order, or moving to his own apartment, or drawing a line in the sand and saying, "Enough is enough. You will not beat me again." So he did what he could.

But now Rick is a thirty-year-old husband and dad. And he is still choosing to lie and pretend, even though it might seem more automatic than a conscious choice. And while those actions served him well with his dad because they helped him to avoid some pain, now they are getting in the way of his relationship with his wife, kids, employer, and friends. These are people who probably would not hurt him for telling the truth—and in fact, *prefer* that he would speak and deal honestly.

In a very real sense, Rick was a victim of his dad. His dad caused Rick injury, and harmed him further by punishing him for telling the truth. The simple truth is that Rick's dad is responsible for his own behavior, and it's not wrong to hold him accountable. But Rick is responsible for Rick's behavior. Rick lies and pretends because of Rick. It would not be healthy or accurate for Rick to say as an adult, "I lie and pretend because of my dad." This is blaming the dad. *This is what's meant by a victim mentality.*

Confronting the Victim Mentality

As we've seen, there is a difference between *blaming* and holding others *accountable* for their behaviors. To blame the past or the people in our past is to say, "I am where I am because of you." This is victim thinking, a victim mentality. This could not be further from the truth. And it could not be more unhealthy.

Here is the truth. We are not where we are in our lives because of what has happened or what others have done to us in the past. We are where we are because of the ways we have chosen to respond to those past events. The "hurters" are responsible for the hurting. But I am responsible for my responses to the hurt. I cannot change what has happened. I cannot change the "hurters." But if I no longer like the ramifications of the choices I made—even though they made sense and seemed like the only alternative at the time—I can make different choices now. *I am responsible.*

The last ten years has seen an outpouring of permission for people to examine their past relationships and to understand how they have been affected by them. Some folks, however, haven't used that permission as an opportunity to learn to make different choices. Instead, they use the past to excuse their present lifestyle, behavior, or poor choices. This is the victim mentality at work.

Recently, there has been a backlash against people with a victim mentality. *Time* magazine had an editorial decrying the fact that Americans are a group of litigious blamers. We blame the people in our lives for our troubles and then sue them. Or we say, "I am not responsible for the murders I just committed because I was abused as a child." At a recent reunion concert, The Eagles, a rock band popular in the late 70s and early 80s, performed a song entitled *Get Over It.* In it they confront the victim mentality that says, "I am where I am because of you, and I can't do anything about it."

Before we jump on this bandwagon, I want to warn you. There is a downside to this backlash. Objections to the continued blaming that comes with a victim mentality has done a great disservice if it prevents legitimate victims from treating their wounds. Of course, there have been Christian counselors and preachers telling believers to "get over it." "Forget what lies behind." "Just pray more." "Read your Bible more." "You shouldn't need counseling to overcome the wounds of the past." In my estimation, this form of Christian "counseling" is shallow and disrespectful of people's pain. It offers hope and healing through "try hard" assignments and exercises, which simply amounts to Christianized behavior modification techniques. It throws out the baby (permission to deal with the wounds and hold the perpetrators accountable) with the bath water (blaming others for our current state and acting powerless to do something about it).

None of this helps either the offender or the victim, both of whom need to differentiate between blame and holding someone accountable. It simply reinforces the idea that talking about the problem causes the problem. And like too many other dynamics in society, it gives victims another reason to choose silence.

Blaming the Victim

Now that you understand that in asking the question I am not trying to cast blame, you can better understand another dynamic: what it means to blame the victim.

Blaming is probably the most prevalent phenomenon that promotes the silence of victims. It also revictimizes them.

A battered wife tells her pastor about her husband's abusive behavior. He says, "George is such a fine man of God. What did you do to provoke it?" Is there ever a good enough reason to beat up your wife?

Victims even blame themselves. Another woman, sexually assaulted on a dark streetside, tells the crisis worker, "I should have known better than to be there at that time of night"—as if she is responsible for the assault. What justifies sexual assault? Being in the wrong place at the wrong time? No. There is no reason good enough. Who is responsible for the assault? The assaulter. Did the victim make a poor choice in the route she chose? Maybe. Can she make a better choice next time? Probably. Does taking responsibility for her choice make her responsible for the assault? No. The attacker is always responsible for the assault.

A friend of mine used to take a blind woman, Cecilia, to the supermarket. One day she left her purse in the cart to go and look at the eggplants. When she came back her purse had been stolen. It was later found, minus cash, in the trash can by the exit. While describing the experience to me she said, "I was so stupid to leave my purse with Cecilia because she can't see." That statement and some others indicated that she was blaming herself. And she was the victim!

I said, "Wait a minute. Who's responsible for your purse getting stolen?"

She said, "I am, because I left it to be guarded by a blind person."

"Wrong," I said. "Why did it get stolen?"

"Because Cecilia was blind and couldn't guard it."

I furrowed my brow at the notion that Cecilia was now responsible.

So she said, "That's wrong, too, isn't it? Well then why?"

"Because there was a thief in the grocery store," I replied. Did my friend make a poor choice about where to leave her purse? Probably. Can she make a better choice next time? Yes. Does taking responsibility for these choices make her responsible, in any way, for the theft? No. The thief is always responsible for the stealing.

Can you see? You can take responsibility for your choices without taking responsibility for the hurtful choices of others. Should you have chosen to stay in that hurtful (dead, irrelevant, unhealthy) church so long? Maybe not. Are you responsible for continuing to pick uncaring, hurtful, or abusive churches? Yes. Can you look at your unhealthy choices and deal with your own inside issues and outside reactions? Can you make better choices about the relationships you pick? Yes. Does taking responsibility for these choices make you responsible, in any way, for the hurtful, neglectful behavior of others? No. The abusers are always responsible for the hurting.

What Are You Responsible For?

Now I am going to take a risk and ask you to consider a tough question: What are you responsible for? I ask *not to blame, but to empower you to change what you can*. Do you believe you are where you are in your relationships to God's people solely because of others? Or can you see that you too have made some choices? And if you no longer like the ramifications of those choices, what different choices can you make?

Let me apply that question in some more practical ways. In Chapter 8, I talked about the "bait and switch." Remember that a spiritual switch takes place whenever there is a substitution of something natural for supernatural, human for divine. Remember, I'm not saying that authority, relationships, or resources are evil. But these things must be utilized in a way that is consistent with the reason God has given them: to serve, equip, and build believers. When they're used this way, the supernatural extends or reaches through the natural, the divine through the human. The result is what Scripture calls the body of Christ. When they aren't used this way, a religious corporation masquerades for the church, and members of the body of Christ are cheated and let down.

Without a doubt, there are many spiritually abused—more than I ever dreamed—who have been baited and switched by others. They have been coerced or browbeaten through the misuse of spiritual authority into building human kingdoms. Where is that sense of blessing they were supposed to experience? It has been lost under the thumb of religious leaders who have misused their authority and defrauded God's own people.

Sometimes We Make the Switch

But not all Christians have been spiritually abused. Some believers settle, all on their own, for a shadow of what is theirs. Why? Because Christians are people who receive life and live life by faith in Someone we cannot see. Yet we are surrounded by objects and people that can be seen, touched, and displayed that promise to meet our needs. And sometimes we forget to fight the fight of faith. When we do forget, we choose to settle for substitutes. In that case, we didn't need coercion or abuse to force us off-track. All we needed was an opportunity. Paul says to the Galatians, "I am amazed that you are so quickly deserting Him who called you by the grace of Christ" (Galatians 1:6).

My point is this: Sometimes we make the "switch" ourselves. We choose to live as if things, people, or behaviors have the power to give us life, value, and acceptance. These have already become ours through our relationship with Christ, but sometimes we forget and make the switch. I know this is true because of being a pastor, counselor, dad, husband, and friend who notices that others do this all the time. *I know this because it's the biggest struggle in my own life! I know this because sometimes I make the switch.*

How about you?

Idolatry

In Chapter 9 we saw that unhealthy relationship skills brought into the church from past relationships are one source of hurt and disillusionment for God's people. A second is idolatry, Scripture's word for making the switch. Whenever we substitute *resources* for the *Source* it is idolatry. Resources, put in the role of the Source, will fail. And when they do, you and I will be let down. It cannot be otherwise.

Idolatry is rampant in the body of Christ. The scary part about it is that the idols in the church *look* spiritual. The end of Galatians 1:6 makes it clear that the believers switched the true gospel for another gospel that really wasn't the Good News. In other words, it looked real but it wasn't.

What are the idols we put in God's role? Paul tells us to rely on God to meet our needs and to enjoy the resources He provides (1 Timothy 6:17). Who or what have we trusted instead to fulfill our expectations? Let's look at a few possibilities:

The Church

We want a fault-proof, totally consistent body of Christ to depend on. But if we stake our faith on it—instead of on God—we will be disappointed.

Other Believers

Christians don't always live like Christians. And we certainly aren't able to perform as perfectly and consistently as God. While this doesn't excuse our behaviors or the hurts we cause, it does explain how the hurts can happen. But are you looking for something to be angry about? Start looking at people. Are you trying to find unfulfillment of your deepest needs? Look at people. Are you needing to feel superior or inferior? Look at someone—anyone else—and opportunities abound.

Ministry

Revelation 2:1–4 says that the church at Ephesus, out of perseverance and zeal for good works and intolerance of anything evil, "left their first love." *Serving* Jesus had replaced Jesus as the focus of their passion.

Our "Equity"

Sometimes the false god we serve in the church is simply all of the time, energy, and money we have already invested. For many people, it's simply easier to stay on the present course and keep investing than it is to step back and consider the possibility that what we're investing in is religious garbage.

Buildings

The church in the United States spends $52 billion a year on mortgage interest. Need I say more?

The Greatest Idol Is Legalism

As in the churches to whom Paul wrote, legalism is the most prevalent, most dangerous, and most easily disguised idol in the church today. It is obsessive perfectionism. It focuses on careful avoidance of certain behaviors. It teaches people to gain a sense of God's acceptance based on their performance of religious duties, instead of continuing to enjoy it as a gift on the basis of Christ.

Legalism permeated the lives and thinking of the believers in the region of Galatia. They had joyously received salvation and their inheritance as heirs of Abraham as a gift. But men from Judea came after Paul to "correct" and supplement his teaching. They said, "Unless you are circumcised according to the custom of Moses, you cannot be saved." In other words, "What Jesus did *plus what you do* is what earns you God's acceptance." (You can read this story and the disciple's response to legalism in Acts 14 and 15.)

In Galatians 3, Paul attempts to awaken the Galatians to the consequences of legalism in their lives. Here's a portion of that confrontation:

> This is the only thing I want to find out from you: did you receive the Spirit by the works of the Law, or by hearing with faith? Are you so foolish? Having begun by the Spirit, are you now being perfected by the flesh? Does He then, who provides you with the Spirit and works miracles among you, do it by the works of the Law, or by hearing with faith? (vv. 2–3, 5)

This is the best example in Scripture of the dynamics of legalism in the lives of individual believers. These folks had begun their journey with God by faith, accepting as a gift what He did through Christ. Then quickly (Galatians 1:6), they turned back again (4:9) to their own religious performance as the measure of God's acceptance and the means to victorious living.

Practically speaking, if you believe that God's ongoing acceptance is based upon the believer's religious behavior, you have to abide by all the correct spiritual p's and q's. And you notice how well others are doing. Measuring your own acceptance based upon performance leads to one of two things: self-righteousness, or a deep sense of shame at not measuring up. Measuring others, furthermore, leads to judgmentalism. This judging of others or being judged by others wounds people and relationships. At Galatia, love had become the casualty of this way of living, to the point that they were on the verge of destruction from "biting" and "devouring [wearing down] one another" (5:15).

In Galatians 5:16–26, Paul describes the true spiritual life in a different way. "Walking by the Spirit"—or continuing to lean on the Spirit as your Source of life, value, meaning, sanctification, and victory—results in changed attitudes and actions. This is love, joy, peace, patience, goodness, kindness, meekness, faithfulness, and self-control. This fruit of the Spirit doesn't result from a believer trying to act spiritual—pasting on a fake smile when you're miserable, for instance, and calling it joy. It doesn't grow by making a checklist to live up to. Instead, Paul has described aspects of a heart-quality that the Spirit produces as we depend upon God. That's why it's called the "fruit of the Spirit"! And when Christians exhibit the fruit of the Spirit, healing and harmony prevail in their relationships with other believers.

"Walking by the flesh"—leaning on or putting faith in what is natural, including positive self-effort—results in an entirely different kind of "fruit": immorality, impurity, sensuality, idolatry, sorcery, enmities, strife, jealousy, outbursts of anger, disputes, dissensions, factions, envyings, drunkenness, carousings, and the like. Legalism makes this a checklist of behaviors to avoid by trying hard. The irony is that leaning on your own self-effort to avoid these behaviors often leads you right into them.

Have you ever been in a group of believers and seen enmities, strife, jealousy, outbursts of anger, disputes, dissensions, factions, and envyings? If you have, then you know how hurtful that can be. Want to know why people have been hurt and let down in so many churches? Believers are walking by the flesh—and they're even doing it in the name of "walking in the Spirit."

Yet we can recognize and take responsibility for the switches we have made in our fight of faith. Only then can we take responsibility to make different choices. Both the false prophets and the Galatians had their part in the Galatians' problem. The false teachers led and they shouldn't have. What they did was wrong. But the Galatians followed. Taking responsibility for our past choices and taking responsibility to now make better ones frees and empowers us to move on.

Paul wrote to tell the Galatians that there were different choices they could make. They could take their eyes off of themselves and others and begin to depend upon God again. In fact, had they remembered this in the first place, they might have gotten a nice letter like the one Paul sent to the Colossians.

Once we have made the switch back, however, there is another fight ahead. We need to learn how to avoid repeating our current difficulties—how to prevent problems before they happen. One of the ways Paul equips believers to avoid making the switch again is by reminding us *who* we are and *whose* we are. We are God's very own sons and daughters, heirs of His great inheritance. It is crucial to know exactly what this means in all its ramifications. And that is the purpose of the next two chapters.

11

Reclaiming Our Spiritual Heritage

When I was a kid one of my favorite shows was the *Twilight Zone*. Some of the episodes were bizarre and others just silly, but there is one episode that sticks out in my memory, perhaps more than any of the others. The sons and daughters of a millionaire gathered for the reading of his last will and testament. The lawyer began the ceremony by showing a movie their father had made before his death. They watched, to their amazement, as he told them all the things he had never said to their faces. He chastised them for their many mistakes and shortcomings. And then, to complete their horror, they discovered that none of them got what they expected and all of them got what they deserved. They had been tricked. They had been cut out of their father's will because they had failed to do what he wanted.

When God's Will Becomes a *Won't*

As followers of Jesus Christ we too have an inheritance: "Also we have obtained an inheritance, having been predestined according to His purpose who works all things after the counsel of His will" (Ephesians 1:11). Unlike the millionaire's unfortunate sons and daughters, it is ours "not on the basis of deeds which we have done in righteousness, but according to [God's] mercy" (Titus 3:5). And again, unlike those ill-fated heirs in the story, we have a Father who is "kind" (Titus 3:4) and "faithful" (1 Corinthians 1:9). He delivers what He promises.

Unfortunately, many Christians have been hurt and disappointed when it comes to their experience as God's family members. As we saw in Part One, they know about the promise of an inheritance, but they feel they have somehow been excluded or missed God's will for them. Listen to some of their stories:

"I am absolutely exhausted from trying to be a 'good' Christian. I don't feel like praying, studying, doing anything I used to do. The most I can do is to tell the Lord how much I love Him. Yet I'm afraid if I don't shape up, the ax is going to fall on my head."

"I was thrilled to accept the grace of God when I first became a Christian, but unless I lived up to the standards imposed by my Christian peers in doctrine, worship, even temperament, I wasn't worthy."

"I've started thinking that this 'Christian stuff' is a bunch of bunk. In fact, I'm teetering on the verge of agnosticism."

"We seem to get out of one abusive church system and into another."

"We are struggling to find out who God really is, what a Christian really is. And we're so tired."

"The joy and freedom in Christ are about gone. Is this really what being a Christian is about?"

Do these sound like the grateful expressions of people who have inherited riches in Christ from their Father in heaven—people who enjoy their inheritance?

Have their experiences among God and His people taught them that His acceptance is based on works? Or that God is kind and merciful—and that there is joy and freedom in the Christian life? These sound more like the testimonies of outcasts, slaves, and black sheep of the family rather than those of heirs to a spiritual fortune.

Reclaiming Our Spiritual Heritage

As we have seen, healing and recovery begins when we reach a point where we take responsibility for our movement from victim to victor. My hope is that you are willing to do that. You will always be faced with accidental hurts, or with people who seem more powerful than you whose actions and attitudes will hurt you. Relationships are risky, and since you live in a world full of fallen people these things are unavoidable.

Nevertheless, there are some things you can do to help prevent the hurts from inflicting devastating damage. I offer these next few chapters to help you create healthy responses to future wounds. For some, this will simply be a matter of remembering *who* you are and *what you have* as a member of God's family. For others, you may be seeing these things for the first time. Either way, understanding this will be liberating to you. And either way, these are things that are yours because you are God's beloved child, fellow-heir with His Son, Jesus Christ.

God's Will

God's will is a phrase that strikes a note of tiredness or confusion in the hearts of many believers. Recently I asked a Christian friend if he would be willing to do a little "word association" exercise. He agreed and I said, "God's will." His responses: *missing it; one perfect thing; unsure; heavy; out of it; getting disciplined.* Notice that he didn't *define* "God's will." Instead, he used words that described more how he *feels* in relationship to it. It all adds up to being *weighed down.*

For most of the Christians I talk to, God's will is a heavy thing. It is His "to do" list, something to figure out. In fact it's something we had better figure out. That's how I thought about it for most of my early life as a believer.

The word translated "will" is the Greek word *thelema*. It means "determination, decree, or purpose." Devoid of context, these meanings do imply a view of God's will as something He wants, a kind of divine wish list for the way things should be. It would be our job as God's followers, then, to discover and follow that list, or to do what God wants.

But there's a different—yet actually quite common—way to think about the word "will." And this gets really exciting when it applies to the will of God. As members of God's family, we are His heirs according to His will. Paul says that God predestined us to become His sons and daughters "through Jesus Christ to Himself, according to the kind intention of His will" (Ephesians 1:5). Though there are several ways people understand the phrase

"God's will" and several ways to understand how it applies to our lives, I'll leave most for a little later in this chapter. For right now let's talk about God's will simply as a "will"—a legal document that sets forth the conditions under which a person's heirs receive their inheritance.

Perhaps you have a will. In our will we have left everything that belongs to us to our four daughters. When we die someday our earthly possessions will be divided among our daughters, our heirs according to our will. If we die before they are adults, our will gives instructions about who should care for our girls and how the resources are to be utilized. But while we are alive—even though our will exists, even though we have named our heirs, and even though what is ours is theirs—our daughters, though always cared for in the present, receive no inheritance. Our will only comes into play when we die.

While many things have changed in the world since the first century, it seems that the basic function of a will has not. Hebrews says,

> For where a covenant is, there must of necessity be the death of the one who made it. For a covenant is valid only when men are dead, for it is never in force while the one who made it lives (9:16–17).

This particular passage is referring to God's last testament: His will. Before the foundation of the world (Ephesians 1:4) God made a will. In His will He left everything to His heirs (Galatians 4:7; Ephesians 3:6). Do you know what He did then? He died! And what happens when the one who made the will dies? The heirs get their inheritance. That's why Ephesians says "We *have obtained* an inheritance" (1:11, italics added).

God's Will in Context

Have you ever thought of God's will like that? This puts it in a whole different light. It isn't just a *little* different than what I had thought—it runs *contrary*. It confronts. Consider for a moment the possibility that, rather than some divine "to do" list, the phrase "God's will" really refers to His last will and testament. In fact, the context of Ephesians 1 shows us that this is exactly the case.

Let me show you what I mean. First, Paul says, "Blessed be the

God and Father of our Lord Jesus Christ, who has blessed us with every spiritual blessing in the heavenly places in Christ" (Ephesians 1:3). The word translated "blessed" is from the Greek word *eulogeo*, which means "to speak well of, prosper or empower." It is the word from which we get our English word "eulogy."

The eulogy is the part of the funeral service when people stand up and "speak well of" their dearly departed uncle who was kind and generous to them as a child, or their mother who made great sacrifices so her children could get an education. Ephesians 1 contains Paul's eulogy of God.

> Blessed be the God and Father of our Lord Jesus Christ, who has blessed us with every spiritual blessing in the heavenly places in Christ, just as He chose us in Him before the foundation of the world, that we should be holy and blameless before Him. In love He predestined us to adoption as sons through Jesus Christ to Himself, according to the kind intention of His will, to the praise of the glory of His grace, which He freely bestowed on us in the Beloved. In Him we have redemption through His blood, the forgiveness of our trespasses, according to the riches of His grace, which He lavished upon us. In all wisdom and insight He made known to us the mystery of His will, according to His kind intention which He purposed in Him with a view to an administration suitable to the fulness of the times, that is, the summing up of all things in Christ, things in the heavens and things upon the earth. In Him also we have obtained an inheritance, having been predestined according to His purpose who works all things after the counsel of His will, to the end that we who were the first to hope in Christ should be to the praise of His glory. In Him, you also, after listening to the message of truth, the gospel of your salvation—having also believed, you were sealed in Him with the Holy Spirit of promise, who is given as a pledge of our inheritance, with a view to the redemption of God's own possession, to the praise of His glory (vv. 3–14).

Remember, out of context, eulogy doesn't necessarily have any connection with someone's death or his last will. For instance, I could eulogize (speak well of) you over lunch. But we are looking at context here. Christ's death has given Paul opportunity to tell of the wonderful ways God's heirs have benefitted because of their relationship with Him.

In fact, notice that the word for "bless" appears two more times in this verse. God "has blessed" (*eulogaisas*) "us with every spiritual blessing" (*eulogia*) "in Christ." This means that our being prospered or empowered by God is a one-point-in-time, completed action. And we have been blessed with every (all, every, the whole, thoroughly) spiritual blessing (empowerment, bounty, or benefit). This verse alone stands as a harsh confrontation of any teaching that says there are things we have to do (like pray, give money, get healed, submit to leaders) in order to somehow get or keep God's blessing.

Named First in the Will

When you were growing up, were you ever picked last? Perhaps the kids in the neighborhood were choosing up sides for a baseball game and you were the last chosen. Or maybe nobody wanted you on their team for the math flash card drill. How did that feel? Awful. I know too many Christians who feel like God's "last picked" because of shaming, rejecting messages they have been given. Or because they don't measure up to someone's performance standards.

Paul tells us in Ephesians 1 that God chose us first, "before the foundation of the world" (v. 4). The verse goes on to say that He did this, "that we should be holy and blameless before Him." A lot of people have learned that verse like this: "He chose us so" we'd better "be holy and blameless." And so the good news of the verse gets lost in our failure to ever be holy and blameless *enough* in order to feel comfortable around God. Literally, the verse says, "His choosing way back then makes us to be holy and blameless now." In other words, it is His choosing us, rather than our behavior, that makes us holy and blameless before Him.

Meeting the "Terms" of the Will

But there were some more terms in God's will that had to be satisfied. Paul tells us that God "predestined us to adoption" into His family "according to the kind intention of His will" (1:5). If we take the word "predestined" out of context and away from its simple meaning—which is "determined ahead of time"—we end up in the theological debate that has raged in the church and divided believers for centuries.

In context we can get a picture of God, Creator and owner of the universe, sitting down and decreeing (before time began) that He wanted everyone who would ever be to be part of His family, according to His purpose, or will. The Greek word *eudokia*, translated "kind intention," also means "good pleasure" or "satisfaction." In this context we see how God is pleased, and how His will is satisfied. And it's not when we figure out what music we can listen to or what school to attend or who to marry. It's when we become His children!

God's Will Delivers Grace

Though you may not have planned on a Greek lesson, I hope you'll stick with me a little longer. What we're about to see has tremendous importance to you.

The next thing Paul tells us are the benefits we, the heirs, receive from the will. The first thing is *charis*—that is, divine acceptance, favor, benefit, pleasure . . . *grace*. It is freely bestowed upon us, and by it we are made to be highly favored. In addition, because of Jesus we have *apolutrosis* ("deliverance" or "full payment"), and *aphesis* ("freedom" and "pardon") from our *paraptomah* (both "unintentional errors" and "willful offenses"). All of this is according to the *ploutos* ("abundance" or "richness") of His *charis* which He *perisseuo* ("superabounded, gave in excess, so much that there was grace to spare").

Now look carefully at the next truths Paul reveals. (We're still in Ephesians 1.) "In wisdom and insight He made known to us the mystery of His will" (1:8, 9). "Made known" is the word *gnorisaso* and it means "to cause to know or to give understanding." Our knowing or understanding God's will is something that God himself brings about and He has already done it. "Making known" His will also satisfies it; the next part of the verse says that He did this "according to His *eudokia*" (satisfaction) "which He *protithemai*" (determined) ahead of time in Christ.

Jesus' death on the cross is what has made all of the resources in God's will available to His heirs. But with any will there must also be someone who administers it. That is why Paul then says that God did this for an "administration suitable to the fullness of the times." The Greek word for administration is *oikonomia*. It means "administrating or dispensing household goods." That is the function of a trustee or executor when it comes time to execute the conditions of a will. This is the person who makes sure the heirs get what is coming to them. Again, this is why Paul says that we, the heirs, have obtained our inheritance (at one point in time, a completed action). He also goes on to say that "God *energeo*"— is always working—"all things according to the *boule*"—counsel or advice—"of His will" (1:11). In other words, any and all of the work that God ever does is simply a matter of Him following the instructions He laid out in His own will ahead of time.

You may also want to read Galatians 4:1–7, where Paul tells us that the "fullness of the time" had come, in which God powered out His grace to us.

Signed, Sealed, and Delivered

Two more words and the Greek lesson is over. Paul says, "In Him, you also, after listening to the message of truth, the gospel of your salvation—having also believed, you were sealed" (one point in time, a completed action done to you) "with the Holy Spirit of promise" (1:13, 14). The kind of "sealed" Paul is talking about is what happens when you use a signet ring to seal a letter closed. For instance, when a king wanted to send an important letter he would drip hot wax on the opening and press his signet—his personalized, identifying mark—into the wax to seal the letter shut. This signified that what the letter contained was private, from the king himself, and should not be tampered with. The royal seal with which we have been marked and sealed is God's own Spirit, "who is given as a *arrhabon*"—valuable commodity given in advance as security for the rest—"of our inheritance."

God determined (willed) ahead of time what we should receive as His heirs and how we should receive it. Then the one who made the will died, the executor of the will dispensed the inheritance to us, and the Holy Spirit sealed the transaction. If you are an heir, you are in God's will and have at your disposal what that will provides.

Have You Lost Your Sense of Blessing?

How many Christians are tiptoeing around trying to be good enough to earn or deserve their own inheritance? You can't deserve or earn the inheritance. Put simply, there are two things that have to be true for a person to be in God's will. If you're a believer, both of them are true concerning you.

The *first* is that you have to become an heir. You did that when you bowed your knee to the Lord. The *second* is that the one who made the will has to die. God did that on the cross 2,000 years ago.

So what went wrong? I think the apostle Paul gives us a hint. He asks, in his letter to the Galatians, "Where, then, is that sense of *makarismos*—blessing, supreme good fortune—you had?" Paul was very concerned about God's heirs in Galatia. It seems to me that Paul would be equally concerned about some of the heirs that live during our time.

Notice that he is not calling into question the *fact* or *reality* of the blessing itself, or whether the Galatians had it. The truth, as he stated in Ephesians 1:11, "we have obtained an inheritance," is that we are not waiting for our inheritance. We already have it. Remember, we have been blessed with every spiritual blessing. Instead, Paul is wondering what caused the Galatians to lose their "sense" or enjoyment of it.

I have talked to so many Christians who have lost—not their blessing, for that cannot be lost—but "that sense" of it. For some it had permeated their relationships with God and others for years—then it disappeared. For others it was a thirty-second rush they felt when they first became a believer—that's it. And now, contrary to the truth about God's blessing, they are haunted by a sense of indictment and doubt: They spend their days thinking, *Did I do something wrong? I thought this was the "gift" of God? What can I do to make it up to you, Lord? Where are you, God? Do you still love me? Am I doing enough? Am I still in your will?*

God's Master "To Do" List

What happened to their sense of being an heir, their sense of Papa God, their sense of God's promise, the sense that filled them with joy and assurance? We have already seen how relating to one another within the body of Christ in unhealthy ways, forgetting who we serve, and building the wrong kingdoms can dampen and even destroy our sense of blessing as God's precious heirs. I'd like to close this chapter by describing how this can happen when we misunderstand what it means to be in God's will and view it as a kind of divine "to do" list.

Have you ever struggled, wondering if you were *in* the will of God? Usually that struggle takes place in one of two ways—trying to know God's will for your life and trying to do the will of God. In order to be *in* God's will you have to *do* His will. And in order to do it you first have to know it. For some believers this causes such anxiety that they try all kinds of methods to figure all of this out.

One of the ways people try to figure out God's will is to "lay out fleeces." It goes something like this: "Lord, if you want me to do thus-and-so, make such-and-such happen." The concept of laying fleeces comes from the story about Gideon in Judges 6. God had told Gideon that He wanted him to fight the Midianites and that He would bring him the victory. But Gideon was afraid and reluctant. So he laid out a piece of wool and asked God to do a miraculous sign with the wool in order to prove He could keep His promise.

There are several versions of the "fleece method" of figuring out God's will—all of them based on some kind of "sign":
- If the money becomes available it must be God's will.
- If there is no resistance or hang-ups—if God doesn't "close any doors"—the Lord must be in it.
- If enough people confirm (or disagree with) what I already suspect to be God's will, then it must (or must not) be God's will.
- If someone recommends the plan out of the blue, or by giving a "word," then it's "of God."
- If I have a dream about it. . . .

The list of methods goes on. At this juncture there are a couple of questions I would like you to consider. First of all, did Gideon lay out the fleece because he wanted to find out what God wanted him to do? No. He already knew what God wanted. Previously, God had said, "Go in this your strength and deliver Israel from the hand of Midian" (Judges 6:14). Was the fleece an example of Gideon's faith in God? No, rather it showed his lack of faith. If you look at the whole story, you will see that even prior to this he had asked God to prove that He was really God by giving him a sign. God did that, and Gideon was finally convinced. But then he wanted to be convinced again (6:36), and again (6:39).

And—back to the fleece—Gideon performed his test twice. I suspect he did that either because he still didn't believe God after the first answer, or because he didn't like the answer he got. The incident sounds a lot like a spiritual version of flipping a coin to make a decision: "Heads I go here, tails I go there." Then if you get the answer you don't really like, you just go for two out of three . . . or five out of nine.

I used to lay out "fleeces"—not to discover if I was in God's will or plan, but to see if God was in mine. I'd already decided what course I wanted to take. I just wanted to see "if the Lord was really in it."

I am not saying that it isn't important for us to make an effort to see or hear what God's will is for us in particular situations. It is in no way inconsistent or unreasonable for us to seek God's leading in our plans and affairs. We love Him, and in our heart of hearts we want what He wants. "I joyfully concur with the law of God in the inner man," says Paul in Romans 7:22. Obedience to Him is simply bringing our outer person in line with our inner heart, home to God's Spirit, the part of us that says "Yes!" to His will and leading.

Neither am I saying that God can't or won't respond to the fleeces we lay out. God can do anything He wants in any way He wants. God responds faithfully even when we don't. He did for Gideon, even though it was doubt, not faith, that motivated Gideon's testing of God. God can and does reveal himself in circumstances—and I think we should keep our eyes, ears, and hearts open for when He does.

When We Don't Know What to Do

What if you don't know what God wills concerning a certain decision? Is it God's will, or preference, you take that job in Wichita Falls—or the one in Walla Walla? It may be that you should wait before you decide. But in those cases where God does have a will, or preference, He is also capable of telling you to wait, or act, in such a way that you can tell it is Him.

But there are other times when you need to use the mind God gave you to pay attention and choose the course that makes the most sense. Maybe in this particular instance God doesn't have a will, or preference, about whether you take the job in Wichita Falls or Walla Walla. So take the job in Wichita Falls if it makes more sense—that is, it's a better job, the schools are better, the benefits are better, the climate is better for your health. In this case God's will, or preference, might simply be that wherever you go, you are to serve Him and be a good steward of the benefits given to you in His will.

In Colossians Paul says, "And whatever you do in word or deed, do all in the name of the Lord Jesus, giving thanks through Him to God the Father" (3:17). And in 1 Corinthians, he says, "Whether, then, you eat or drink or whatever you do, do all to the glory of God" (10:31). Do these things in Wichita Falls *or* Walla Walla. Live like an heir and be a good steward of your inheritance wherever you are. It will "speak well of" your Father.

Why Do We Fear?

For some believers, trying to discern God's will isn't just a matter of loving God and seeking His loving purposes for their lives. They do it out of fear and questions of whether His love and acceptance will remain. What if they make a mistake? As I said before, some see God's will as a not-yet-discovered "to do" list. Or as a divine multiple-choice test where there is only one right answer. If they misread the signals and guess *A* when the answer is really *B*, they will miss God's will. They will fail the test. Or they will wander around in plan B—which is second-best—instead of plan A—which is perfect. In other words, they will be stuck with God's "permissive" will instead of His "perfect" will. Or they'll be outside of His will altogether.

There are others who are so paralyzed by the fear of making a mistake that they don't make choices at all. For many believers, mistakes in relationships have resulted in hurt. Mistakes have led to being rejected. Relationships have fallen apart because of mistakes. That's what experience has taught many in the church.

But this isn't so with God. Paul says, "You have not received a spirit of slavery leading to fear again, but you have received a spirit of adoption as sons [and daughters] by which we cry out, 'Abba! Father!' " (Romans 8:15). Paul also asks, "Who shall bring a charge against God's elect?" No one! "God is the one who justifies; who is the one who condemns?" No one! "Who shall separate us from the love of Christ?" No one, and nothing!

Can misreading God or making a mistake separate us? What do you think?

So what if you get to Wichita Falls and find out that God really willed (preferred) for you to go to Walla Walla after all? If that happens, change your mind and plans and go to Walla Walla. "Papa" God will be there with you too. Go in the name of Jesus. And live there to the glory of God. There are folks in Walla Walla who need to meet this Father you "speak of so well."

Our Heritage as Recipients of God's Will

Paul used the first part of Ephesians 1 to elaborate on what it means to be sons and daughters of God. He closes the chapter by letting them in on one of the prayers he prays for them:

> For this reason I . . . do not cease giving thanks for you, while making mention of you in my prayers; that the God of our Lord Jesus Christ, the Father of glory, may give to you a spirit of wisdom and of revelation in the knowledge of Him. I pray that the eyes of your heart may be enlightened, so that you may know [always be sure of] what is the hope of His calling, what are the riches of the glory of His inheritance in the saints, and what is the surpassing greatness of His power toward us who believe (vv. 15–19).

Paul wants the Ephesians to be sure of and to remember what is true about them because of what God has done. He even implores God to bring that about.

I want to remind you, once again, who you are and what is yours as God's heir. As I do that, it's my hope that your sense of knowing what God has already made known won't depend upon the words on these pages. My prayer is that God, who has already given everything else, might give you a spirit of wisdom and revelation and knowledge of Him at this moment.

So much more than a divine "to do" list, God's will is really His divine *gift* and *resource* list. God's will provides us with the resources we need to live the lives, have the families, raise the children, do the ministry, that would "speak well of" Him.

It's Our Heritage . . .

. . . to know God as our "Abba, Father." Many people relate to God as kind of a fickle adolescent whose well-being, moods, and views of them depend upon their performance. They live as if they have the power to control God. But it is God who is the powerful One. He has used His power to taste and to overcome death on our behalf. And He left a last will and testament in which He named us as family members. By this will he brought us into His family. And through it He lavished upon us a rich inheritance. To those of us who are His heirs, He is not a judge to fear but a Papa in whose household we can be safe and be sure that we belong.

... to know who we are. As God's sons and daughters we are loved and accepted, forgiven, redeemed, washed, sanctified, justified, blessed with every spiritual blessing, chosen, adopted. We are His workmanship, fellow citizens of His kingdom and fellow partakers with Jesus of His promises. We are a fragrant aroma to Him, a chosen race, a royal priesthood, holy brethren, His very own people. In Him we have been made complete, and He's the One who decides that (See Colossians 2:10).

... to be led by Him. His Spirit lives in us and is capable of communicating His concerns and direction. Sometimes He does it through His Word. Sometimes through circumstances. And sometimes through people who are wise and good at listening to God.

Remember, the will of other well-meaning Christians is not necessarily the same thing as God's will. We serve *Him*—and not as paupers, slaves, or people-pleasers. We serve because we are free to enjoy our inheritance. And because of that, we can become liberal caterers to the lost, spreading for them the banquet of spiritual blessings that God has set before us.

Once we know *this* view of God's will, we are on the move to a new place in spirit—a place where legalism, manipulation, rejection, and disapproval lose their deadening power. We are headed to the experience of freedom in Christ.

12

Standing Firm in Freedom

Recently I received this letter from Ben in Massachusetts:

> I received Jesus as my Savior at age fifteen. I was *filled with peace, liberation, and joy.* Then someone in our church gave me a set of cassette tapes by a legalist preacher. Many people in the church had already adopted his legalistic attitudes and set about shaming me into cutting my hair, wearing certain clothes, and following other standards equated with holiness. *All the joy and freedom in Christ were gone* (emphasis mine).

In the previous chapter we saw that our Father's birthing, adopting, and choosing us means we were never meant to live as outcasts of God's family. You and I are not meant to live like second-class citizens of God's kingdom. We are sons, daughters, and heirs of an almighty Father. But living like inferior or disenfranchised family members is not the only way our spiritual wounding cripples us. Like Ben, many of us have lost our sense of spiritual freedom. We have learned to live like slaves, not the "free and willing followers of Jesus," but of others.

Serving One Master

In 1 Corinthians the apostle Paul says,

> For he who was called in the Lord while a slave, is the Lord's freedman; likewise he who was called while free, is Christ's slave. You were bought with a price; do not become slaves of men (7:22–23).

This passage presents believers with vital truth. We belong to

153

Christ. He bought us, and we are now free to choose Him as our only Master—to become "slaves" to the One who frees us. A slave to spiritual freedom in Christ—what a great form of "slavery"!

Based upon our spiritual freedom we are to see in every relationship with other human beings the possibility of serving Him. We are not meant to become slaves of other people. Paul, in fact, goes so far as to say that trying to please others, or to gain their favor, is in direct opposition to being a slave of Christ (See Galatians 1:10).

Even though he had set his heart to serve Jesus, Ben's heart was conscripted by the people of his church and the teaching of that pastor—shanghaied, so to speak. He was kidnapped and fell into bondage to people, to their opinions and their sense of what constituted holiness. Christians robbed Ben of "that sense of blessing" he once had, that sense that Paul warned us not to lose (See Galatians 4:15).

Being a slave of the *right* Master, Jesus, produces one of the great benefits of the Christian life: freedom from lesser masters—including legalism, and the opinions and lifestyle choices based on other people's consciences. Once again, remember the word "slave," *doulos*, means "bond-servant"—someone who has willingly sold themselves into servitude for some higher gain or benefit, not someone who was dragged away as a captive slave. The concept of *doulos* is that we have freedom of choice.

Now some argue that Paul says we have been *bought*—which seems to indicate we don't have a choice. Therefore, they say, we really aren't free, just slaves of a different master. But in the same passage, Paul also tells us not to become slaves of men. That warning and command makes no sense if we have no real choice about whom we will serve. So even in our *bought-with-a-price* condition, we are free to choose. I believe it must be so because of the nature of the One who bought us.

Paul says that God sent His Son,

> . . . in order that He might redeem *esxagorazo*—"buy back," "pay a ransom" those who were under the Law, that we might receive the adoption as sons. And because you are sons, God has sent forth the Spirit of His Son into our hearts, crying, "Abba! Father!" Therefore you are no longer a slave, but a son; and if a son, then an heir through God (Galatians 4:5–7).

Jesus doesn't buy us out of slavery to make us slaves. Instead, our new master releases us to live as free sons and daughters, as heirs. "It was for freedom that Christ set us free" (Galatians 5:1).

There are many profound paradoxes in the Christian life. He who has found his life shall lose it, but he who has lost his life shall find it (Matthew 10:39). The first will be last, and the last first (Matthew 19:30). The greatest will be the servant of all (Matthew 23:11). Everyone who exalts himself shall be humbled, and he who humbles himself shall be exalted (Luke 14:11). Add to these: *The way to have freedom is to become a slave.*

My First Opportunity to Return to Slavery

I am a graduate of Bethel College in St. Paul, Minnesota. Bethel was the fourth college I attended, and I went there only after my life had been heaved upside-down. It was there I met Jesus Christ. It was there I saw for the first time a gathering of Christians who truly loved each other. And they loved me—for free. This contradicted most of what I had experienced until then. Sure, I'd been loved by believers prior to this point. And I'd seen believers who loved Jesus. But by and large, my experience of professing Christians was that they majored on the minors—carefully straining out the gnats of long hair and music with a beat, but swallowing the camels of backbiting, gossip, and hypocrisy.

It was also at Bethel that I grew a beard. On my first visit home from Bethel, I was looking for an item for school at the department store where most people in our area did their shopping. Out of the corner of my eye I noticed that someone was staring at me from farther down the aisle. I turned my head, and to my horror I saw that Mrs. Dodge had zeroed in on me (Dodge wasn't her real name, but I'll call her that because "dodge" is what I wanted to do when I saw her coming).

Mrs. Dodge was one of the most openly critical people in my church, a master with the spiritual stiletto. In one or two sentences she could lay you wide open with a barrage of "loving" insults. I'd seen many of her prey left in a bleeding daze as she walked away smiling. She was the spiritual equivalent of a drive-by shooting. Most other people in my church actually *thought* like Mrs. Dodge, but she was the self-appointed hit man for what others were too gutless to say.

When I saw her in the department store I called out, "Hello, Mrs. Dodge. Happy Easter."

She wheeled and came toward me, her face already puckering. "*What* have you *done* to yourself?" she lashed out. Some Easter greeting.

"What do you mean?" I gulped.

"Your *face!*" she said bitterly.

"I grew a beard. What's wrong with that?" Why I asked, I'll never know. I guess I didn't feel skewered enough.

She smiled, shook her head in utter disapproval, turned her back to me and walked away. I was dismissed.

I was also hurt. Now it would have been a simple matter if it was just that Mrs. Dodge didn't like my beard. That's life. Had the mother of one of my non-Christian friends said exactly the same thing, it would only have meant "I don't like your beard." Some people don't like beards. I knew what the verbal assault was really about. As I explained before, I had grown up in a hyper-judgmental spiritual context, the kind that spawns the Mrs. Dodges of the world. In this context facial hair is not a matter of personal taste— it's a spiritual issue. And once something is deemed a spiritual issue, it somehow gives people the right to question another person's relationship with God. In that brief exchange I knew I was viewed as a second-class citizen in the eyes of people in my own "home church"—spiritually unacceptable.

Conformity . . . or Hostility

As Mrs. Dodge walked away I scrambled in my mind to justify myself. *What have I done to myself? Well, I quit using drugs. I moved away from all my negative friends. I enrolled in a Christian college. I found the Lord, for Pete's sake!*

In the past when I had felt pressure by the religious crowd to measure up to a certain standard, I simply caved in. It wasn't *obedience*—it was *expedience*. I didn't have the inner resources to do anything but conform to the pressure to act religious. I was nothing but a doormat with a big Christian fish painted on it. And I attempted to salve my insecurity with religious, approval-seeking actions and behaviors.

But this time it was different. I had a different reaction to the pressure. I became very defensive.

After I got through shoring up my own inner protective walls by scrambling to justify my new "freedom," I went on the attack. Because she had attacked me I felt justified in attacking her. Inwardly I began to seethe, and in addition to the word "legalist," I picked up other mental rocks to throw at Mrs. Dodge—silently, of course. She was, without argument, sloppy in appearance. You can imagine what I did with that fact. In order to "protect" my freedom I attacked her viciously, even though I never said a word out loud.

It's obvious to me now that even though I had become a Christian, I really hadn't grown much in the inner-resource department. I was as insecure as ever. Hostility, like conformity, is a sin. Both miss God's mark, which is standing our ground as believers who are free in Christ.

I know the incident with Mrs. Dodge would not have been that big a deal for someone who was securely grounded in their faith, someone who had a firm grasp of their identity. But for me—a new believer with a history of spiritual insecurity—it was a huge deal. I am years down the path from that place in my journey of faith, and have a much clearer understanding of who I am in Christ. But I face frequent opportunities to return to the bondage of measuring up. The temptations to get hostile or insecure haven't ceased either. If anything, the struggle has intensified.

Regardless of the pressure, though, we don't have to give in to mere external conformity and shrink into compliant religious performance. Neither do we need to attack those who insinuate negative things about us as believers. There is a third alternative.

Standing Firm

Paul says,

> It was for freedom that Christ set us free; therefore keep standing firm and do not be subject again to a yoke of slavery (Galatians 5:1).

We can stand firm.

In the letters Paul wrote, he gave advice on certain pressing issues in the lives of the churches, encouraging believers in some areas, confronting them in others. In Galatians and Colossians, perhaps more than in his other letters, Paul addressed the importance of standing firm in the faith.

But there is a big difference between the two books. Galatians carries an angry tone, and was written to confront Christians in Galatia (probably four churches in a region of Asia Minor). When Paul was there in person, he'd preached God's grace to people who were exhausted from trying to appease their former pagan gods. He told them of a new open route to God—*faith in Jesus Christ*. They had received that Good News with joy.

But certain people followed behind Paul everywhere he went to "correct" or "complete" his message. These "Judaizers" believed that unless a believer was circumcised according to the custom of Moses, he couldn't be saved (Acts 15:1). They added human good works to Christ's work of the cross as the way to earn God's acceptance. In Acts 15:5 we read:

> But certain ones of the sect of the Pharisees who had believed, stood up, saying, "It is necessary to circumcise them, and to direct them to observe the Law of Moses."

Some believers, right there in Christianity's home base, didn't believe that faith in Christ was enough.

"Don't get us wrong," they were saying. "It's not that faith in Christ isn't *important*, it's just that it *isn't enough*." That's the message the Galatians had bought into. They had begun their lives with God by faith. But they started measuring their ongoing *spiritual acceptability to God* by the ruler of their adherence to certain religious codes of outward conduct. And so they were trying to complete with their own good works what God had begun with His Spirit. Paul compared what had happened to having a spell cast on them (3:1), raising the concern that perhaps they had never been saved in the first place (4:11). He called the legalists "Ishmaels" (4:22–31), the ultimate insult to a Jew. He even went so far as to say that he wished the Judaizers would just castrate themselves—in essence, if you're going to try to win God's favor by cutting something off, you had better keep cutting (5:12).

A Preemptive Strike

In contrast, Paul's letter to the Colossians is far different. It's a kinder, gentler letter. First, he acknowledges the Colossians' unshakable faith in Christ. It's important to know that the same false Judaizing message had been preached to them. But they had not given in. So Paul praised them, saying,

> For even though I am absent in body, nevertheless I am with
> you in spirit, rejoicing to see your good discipline and the sta-
> bility of your faith in Christ (Colossians 2:5).

In other words, "You Colossians do a really good job of holding on to Jesus. You haven't gotten sidetracked."

Second—and equally important—Paul launches in the letter to the Colossians a "preemptive spiritual strike" on behalf of God's grace. He bolsters the faith of the Colossians—and our own—to withstand attacks that will come from those who would teach that a living, active faith in Christ isn't enough.

The preemptive strike is found in Chapters 2 and 3 of Colossians, and it comes in five waves. There are four "don'ts" and one "do." Here they are:

"Don't be taken captive" (2:8).

"Let no one act as your judge" (2:16–17).

"Let no one defraud you" (2:18–19).

"Don't submit to human precepts" (2:20–23).

"Keep holding on to life in Jesus" (2:6–8 and 3:1–2).

In these chapters Paul also includes several explanations as to what will happen to the Colossians if they fail to heed his advice. As I address each of these passages, I will explain the meaning of the phrases, then place them in the context of the spiritual struggle that the Colossians faced—the struggle that we ourselves must face.

Don't Be Taken Captive

> See to it that no one takes you captive through philosophy
> and empty deception, according to the tradition of men, ac-
> cording to the elementary principles of the world, rather than
> according to Christ.

Paul warns us of this danger in Colossians 2:8. As we have already seen, we have freely given ourselves to be slaves of Christ. Paul reminds us there is a difference between being a *doulos* and being taken as a captive. Paul isn't at all concerned about being taken captive to Christ—because captives of Christ are growing in spiritual freedom from both law and sin.

The word that is translated "taken captive" is *sulagogeo*. It describes a kind of kidnapping, a situation in which *we* are the booty, like being born into a great family—which we have been—and then being stolen away from your real parents, in our case, Christ. That's why in the next five verses the phrases *in Him, with Him, of Him, through Him* appear eight times. Paul is reminding us *whose* we really are.

On TV dramas the villains sometimes induce a stupor in the victim before snatching him or her away. They slip a "mickey" to the victim in a drink that looks safe—a glass of milk, for example. In Colossians Paul is talking about a spiritual kidnapping. In this abduction of the spirit, the spiritual "mickey" comes in two "drinks," both of which look safe. One is philosophy or sophistry. Paul is referring to a form of Jewish philosophy, according to *Strong's Concordance*. The second is outright deceit. The reason I include deceit in the "looks safe" category is because that's the nature of deceit. It sounds so good that you don't know you're being deceived. If you did know, you wouldn't allow yourself to be deceived.

The text indicates that in this spiritual kidnapping, the kidnappers "bewitch" (Paul's word in Galatians 3) their victims. They do this by drugging them, as it were, with the "traditions of men," which means Jewish traditionalistic law—again, according to *Strong's Concordance*. The Judaizers were trying to get the Colossians to swallow their teaching that right standing with God was found in the cross of Christ *plus* . . .

The other "drug" is the "the elementary principles of the world." Simply put, the basic principles of every thought system in the world—with the exception of Christianity—is that life, value, and meaning come from a person's behavior and achievement.

This is why Paul says, "In Him you have been made complete, and He is the head over all rule and authority" (Colossians 2:10). In other words, you don't have to do anything to *fill* yourself. You are full *in Christ*, and He has the final word. Neither do you have to vindicate yourself (vv. 11–14), because He has removed all charges against you. Living as if these statements are fact will keep you out of slavery.

Don't Let Anyone Judge You

Paul then says,

> Therefore let no one act as your judge in regard to food or

drink or in respect to a festival or a new moon or a Sabbath day—things which are a mere shadow of what is to come; but the substance belongs to Christ (Colossians 2:16–17).

Paul is saying, literally, to "keep letting no one judge you," because fending off judgment is going to be an energy-consuming, ongoing battle. In Galatians 4:10 we read that the Galatians were observing special days, seasons, and events, and judging themselves spiritually superior because of it. In contrast, it's apparent that the Colossians were *not* observing these rituals. As far as Paul is concerned, these things are just a shadow, and the Colossians were holding on to the real source of life—Jesus Christ. And he warns that there will always be someone tempting them to let go of the *real thing*, which can't be seen, and grab on to the *shadow*, which can. And what powers this temptation is that they will be judged spiritually inferior if they refuse.

I suppose this could be compared to being informed by an attorney that someone has left you a huge sum of money. The catch is that you have to wait quite a while before it's actually at your disposal. So in lieu of the total amount, you could have twenty-five percent now. Do you take what you can see (a "bird in the hand"), or do you wait for what you can't?

In a practical sense, perhaps this is why believers sometimes get more enamored with their pastor, or a church building, or successful programs, than with Jesus.

Now let me tell you what this *doesn't* mean. "Let no one act as your judge" doesn't mean that we shouldn't allow anyone to confront us about our real mistakes, failures, and sins. We are accountable to God and to each other for the way we live. Our behavior affects everyone around us, and we need the warnings, encouragements, and instructions of others so that we can learn to make better choices about how to live.

Don't Let Anyone Cheat You

Paul's warning continues:

Let no one keep defrauding you of your prize by delighting in self-abasement and the worship of the angels, taking his stand on visions he has seen, inflated without cause by his fleshly mind, and not holding fast to the head, from whom the entire body, being supplied and held together by the joints and ligaments, grows with a growth which is from God (Colossians 2:18–19).

Paul adds urgency to this last section with the Greek word *medeis*, which means "no way, and without delay." Add this to Paul's imperative and you get "keep letting no one cheat you out of your prize, starting immediately."

Have you ever felt disqualified as a believer? Perhaps you have had a certain problem "good" Christians aren't supposed to have. Or you couldn't seem to get a situation under control as fast as other people thought you should. Or your experience of the Holy Spirit doesn't measure up to the experience fellow church members talk of. Disqualification is what these verses talk about. Don't let anyone cheat you out of your prize by telling you that you don't qualify, that you don't deserve it. The way they try to do this is to point at the things that qualify them. They delight in self-abasement, translated from a Greek word that means "humility." Have you ever known someone who acts like they get points with God based upon how humble they are—puffed up about how *unpuffed up* they are?

But they're puffed up in vain, because the basis of their spiritual qualification is all of the religious experiences they have had or how intellectually perceptive they believe themselves to be, not the *real* basis of holding fast—or "strongly seizing"—God: the grace of God in Christ.

Don't Submit to People Prescriptions

Paul's final salvo comes in Colossians 2:20–23. His fourth "don't" really comes in the form of the question:

If you have died with Christ to the elementary principles of the world, why, as if you were living in the world, do you submit yourself to decrees, such as, "Do not handle, do not taste, do not touch!" (which all refer to things destined to perish with the using)—in accordance with the commandments and teachings of men? These are matters which have, to be sure, the appearance of wisdom in self-made religion and self-abasement and severe treatment of the body, but are of no value against fleshly indulgence.

Why do you place yourselves under the prescribed religiosity of people? he asks. Stop it.

I believe this passage reveals something of terrific importance and power. I want to take some time to explain it to you.

After saying that no one is to judge us or cheat us of our spiritual inheritance, you might think that Paul would also issue a counter-balance warning about the evils of the flesh. You might think he would say something like, "If you have died with Christ to the ABC's of the world—which are that sex, money, drugs, or religion can give you life—why do you still live like the world does? Why do you handle, taste, and touch things that have no power to give you life?" Another way to say it might be: "If you have life in Jesus, why do you still try to get life from things that can't give it?" A still more practical way to phrase it: "If you have life in Christ, and no longer get value and meaning from sex," (the example I'll use from here on) "why do you still pursue sex in the same way that you did before you were a Christian—that is, as a 'proof' that you are loved or powerful?" These are legitimate and helpful questions to someone struggling with sex.

But this is NOT what Paul asks. Instead he asks, "Then why do you follow *rules* regarding these things?" Remember, the Colossians were not at this moment in danger of being taken captive by an obvious misuse of something like sexuality, which is the experience of some people. But they were in danger of losing their freedom to *religion*. That is why the question refers to the rules.

So here's the progression of Paul's thinking, as I understand it:

1. You used to live as if you believed that something like sex had power to meet your needs.

2. Then you came to believe that the only real power to give life was Jesus Christ.

3. If that is where the power is, why would you then act as if your only hope against being trapped in an unhealthy pursuit of sex is to make a rule against it?

4. So, just do what you did in the first place, keep your faith in Jesus to meet your needs.

He is saying, "Struggling to live up to or control yourself with a rule has no power to validate you, fulfill you, or to meet your needs. Keeping a rule is just as weak and ineffective in meeting your real need for spiritual life as giving in. Both are empty. Instead, keep drawing life from Christ.

Picture This

Let me paint a couple of word pictures for you. Once there was an orchard with all sorts of wonderful fruit growing in it. The owner had constructed a fence around it to keep people out. On all four corners were posted "NO TRESPASSING" signs. Whenever you passed by you would think about how good it would be to have some of the fruit. Eventually you decided that you had to have some of that fruit, it looked so good. So you dug a hole under the fence, climbed through, and took some of the produce. You were a trespasser. Then one day the Lord came along, driving a produce truck. You noticed that the fruit in the orchard paled in comparison to what the Lord had on His truck. He invited you to hop in, which you did, and He offered to share His fruit with you. He even said He had made you part-owner in His farm. Are you now going to jump out of the truck and build a higher fence around the neighbor's land to keep you from trespassing on that forbidden ground? The presence of a fence, signs and all, didn't have the power to keep you out of that orchard before.

As believers we have received our lives by the same power that raised Christ from the dead. We are dead to the ABC's of the world, knowing they cannot meet our need for life within. But there are three more reasons for believers not to trust in the power of rules for victory in the Christian life. First, the Colossians were told the observance of certain rules was necessary to ground them firmly in the Christian life. But as we see, there is a danger of being led as captives away from Jesus through emphasizing observance of human rules, even if they are clothed in religion. Second, we "have already been firmly rooted and are now being built up in Him and established in your faith" (Colossians 2:7). We cannot complete with our self-effort what was begun by God through our faith (Galatians 3:1–5).

And there is a third reason. While having rules and trying to follow them looks good, *it doesn't work.* In other words, when we pursue sinful sexual behavior we act as if sex has the power to give us the meaning, worth, and life we are hungering for. When we construct a hedge around sinful sexual behavior, we act as if rules have power. Here's the irony: In relying on tougher rules we actually pay homage to sex, acknowledging its power rather than Christ's.

Admittedly, a rule-keeping strategy for Christian living "speaks of wisdom in self-made religion, self-abasement, and severe treatment of the body" (Colossians 2:20–22). Consequently, it will look good to the religious crowd. But while self-made religion (literally, "will-worship," or relying on self-will to gain the victory), self-abasement (lowliness of mind), and severe treatment of the body (self-neglect), look good, they are *of no value against fleshly indulgence.*

Rules have no power.

With this mind, it's possible that what looks like some great victory by some great Christian is simply the result of relying on a strong will instead of a strong God. And what supplants the true humility that comes from resting in Christ is an attempt to earn points with God by "dying to self" well enough.

Instead . . . Hang On to Jesus

So, stay in the truck with Jesus, keep enjoying what He supplies, and—now that you have ownership in the farm—go learn about being a farmer. Or, as Paul said when he praised the Colossians: "As you therefore have received Christ Jesus as Lord, so walk in Him" (2:6). This means "keep walking, and walking, and walking, and walking" as you did in the first place—*by faith.* You came by faith, you were "firmly rooted" by it, you are being built and established by it, so keep walking in it.

Paul also says, "Keep seeking the things above, where Christ is, seated at the right hand of God. Set your mind on the things above, not on the things that are on earth" (Colossians 3:1–2). Your life comes from a spiritual source, Christ himself. Keep looking there to be fulfilled, instead of looking around at all the things that promise to fill you but can't.

Many of us have been let down in our relationships with others. The messages we received through these experiences paralyzed us or robbed us of our freedom as believers. Remembering our identity and heritage as God's sons and daughters makes it possible for us to stand our spiritual ground against these debilitating messages.

From this place of strength in God, we can recover from the wounds incurred in relationships with other members of God's family. In this strength, we can risk building relationships once again, and that is where we now turn our attention.

13

The Four R's of Recovery

Several years ago, I began feeling considerable pain in my lower back, similar to a pain I had experienced on several occasions in the past. On each of those occasions the problem ran its course and the pain eventually subsided. This time the pain stayed and grew worse. I discovered that a disc had become herniated, gradually ballooning out from between the vertebrae. After a couple of months it actually ruptured, and I was in excruciating pain. So it was off to the hospital for major surgery.

After some days recuperating in the hospital, I went home with instructions from my doctor to spend the next six weeks resting. I was supposed to undertake only minimal movement to and from the lying-down position. Even those times when I decided to get out of bed or off the sofa, Holly had to be there to help support me. I wasn't bothered too much by my limitations, however—because I didn't *want* to do anything!

Eventually, moving from place to place became easier as my condition improved. My muscles slowly began to grow strong again, simply because I was using them. And there were some reasons why I wanted to aggressively rebuild my strength. First, prior to my surgery I was so preoccupied with my back pain I had failed to notice something that was so obvious afterward. Because my nerves were so compromised, the calf muscle in my left leg had all but disappeared. In fact, there was a hollow spot where the muscle used to be. In that condition my leg wasn't much more than a pole off of which I pushed in order to walk. I was horrified, and I wanted to regain the strength in that leg as soon as possible. Second, I wanted to build up muscles that would help protect my back from injury in the future.

At my two-month follow-up visit with the doctor, I asked him to suggest an exercise program. He did, and I left feeling motivated and hopeful. Encouraging as that visit was, my next visit was equally disheartening. This time, the doctor told me some of the things I should never do again. Part of the list was quite humorous. I should never plan on skydiving. I hadn't considered taking that up in the past, and it wasn't one of my future goals, either. That was also true of bull-fighting, mountain climbing, and Australian Rules football, which were now "forbidden." But he also mentioned things that were really important to me—paddling a canoe, racquetball, certain strenuous activities associated with hunting and fishing, and most lifting. As Holly and I left the office that day, I turned to her and said, "I *never* expected to have a conversation like that at thirty-eight years of age."

I plunged into a well of grieving, surpassed in depth and darkness only by the sorrow I felt at the time of my father's death. By the time I reached home, I had *catastrophized* most of what I had been told. In my mind "limited lifting" turned into *I'll never be able to twirl my grandchildren in the air.* (I didn't even have any!) And *I'll never be able to go hunting or fishing again.* Plus my involvement with sports would be confined to spectating. My days of participating were over.

It took quite a while after receiving that news for me to actually begin the exercises my doctor prescribed. I was so afraid of reinjuring my back—because I didn't ever again want to hurt as badly as I had—that I put off doing the thing I needed to do most. What I *wanted* to do was lie around and grieve. What I *needed* to do was tax myself, move around, loosen up.

Eventually I decided to take a chance and begin exerting myself. I discovered something. My fear was for nothing. I was careful and did *not* hurt my back. Exercise actually made my back feel better, even when I was at rest. It is true that I have had to let go of some things—lifting, mostly. But through careful rehabilitation, I have safely reclaimed a number of the hobbies and activities important to me. I'm also able to do some things I wasn't supposed to be able to do—paddle a canoe, twirl my niece and nephew. Beyond that, the experience has actually provided an opportunity to try out new activities that might rejuvenate me.

What I Noticed in Rehab

I have learned a lot through the process of being functional, to being out of commission, to being in commission again. For instance, I spend a lot of time reminding believers that it's okay to need help and ask for it. We don't lose points with God for having needs. God's acceptance of us is based upon what Jesus did on the cross, not on whether or not we have problems or struggles. Yet I also noticed just how indicted I feel personally for needing help.

Prior to surgery, if I was carrying boxes and someone offered to open a door for me, I said, "No, I can get it." Somehow I would get that door open myself. It would often be a struggle, but I would manage. As the pain gradually increased I let others open the door. Eventually I had to ask someone to open the door—but at least I could carry boxes. Now I have to ask people to carry the boxes. I *hate* that. Everything inside me says, *I'm not supposed to need help.* But the truth is out: Sometimes, many times, I do need help.

I also noticed that recovery is definitely a *process.* It takes time. It doesn't happen overnight. It doesn't happen on command. And it doesn't happen according to other people's schedules. In the past several years people have shared with me many stories of recovery—physical, emotional, spiritual. I have noticed that there are several common factors in people's recovery processes. I think of these factors as the four R's of recovery: *Rest, Rehabilitation, Release,* and *Risk.*

1. Rest

As with any wound, the emotional and spiritual damage incurred in our relationships with God's people requires an initial period of rest, like it or not. Frankly, many people don't like it. In most of the letters I receive concerning this issue, people report that they found themselves in an uncomfortable, unfamiliar period of what I would call resting from religious people and activities. They are resting from "church."

> I never thought I would have to take a stand for my spiritual and emotional health by not going to church. It has been a scary, uncomfortable time. But I have found that I am free to love and worship Jesus, unencumbered by the weight of endless religious activity.

I have a deep walk with the Lord Jesus, but I find that dealing with "church" is hard. I avoid anyone that reminds me of my previous church experience.

It seems like I am on a sort of "forced leave of absence" from God. While this is rather terrifying for me (I'm kind of sitting around waiting for lightning to strike), I just can't bring myself to go near church, any church. I want to, but I can't.

I know that I need to get over how I'm feeling pretty quickly and get back to church, or God's going to have my neck.

As you can see in the first excerpt, the person has equated church with "the business of doing things in God's name." In the second instance, church equals "the people who go to church." In the third instance, "not going to church" is equated with "being absent from God." The last person feels not just apart from God, but at odds with God. In every example the person is uncomfortable with his current state, and the last person is even a bit panicky.

I can only speculate why resting is so hard for people. What I have learned through my periods of inactivity is that I have a need to be needed. I feel good when I am the one called upon to contribute. In itself this isn't a bad thing. But it crosses a line when my contributing provides me with a way to medicate the sense of empty worthlessness going on inside me, or a way to ignore what is going on around me.

If you find yourself in a period of inactivity, forced or voluntary, don't panic. You don't have to "fix" it by quickly finding something to do. God doesn't love you any less because you aren't performing. Instead, look and listen inside. Has your busyness prevented you from feeling how hurt, angry, or depressed you are? If you're not busy, do you feel like you have lost God's approval? Have you drowned out God's still voice of comfort—His approval—in the rush of your activity to please Him? Why is it so hard for you to do nothing? There are a lot of questions to ask, a lot of insights to be gained during this time. This isn't a wasted period of time, it's a journey.

Learn to listen to the *outside* as well. The struggles we have endured in our relationships with other believers rarely go unnoticed. Caring friends, co-workers, and concerned family members have quite likely been observing our struggle. They have noticed our weary disillusionment. They may have felt our pain and tried to help—but we could not hear what they had to say. Voices of concern may have been swallowed up in our flurry of activity as we tried to make the system work. Or we silenced them by defending the very religious systems that exhausted us, or we punished others for noticing our weakness. We justified our cover-up with Bible verses. But now, while all the activity has ceased, pay attention to any and every person who genuinely cares about you. You'll know them by this trait: They have no agenda, no checklist, and no image to build. They are just concerned for you.

Those seemingly broken-down times provide us with an opportunity to find who our real support people are. I call them the "Tituses." In 2 Corinthians 1:3, 4, Paul says, "Blessed be the God and Father of our Lord Jesus Christ, the Father of mercies and God of all comfort; who comforts us in all our affliction." Much later, he reveals one of the ways God comforts. "For even when we came into Macedonia our flesh had no rest, but we were afflicted on every side: conflicts without, fears within. But God, who comforts the depressed, comforted us by the coming of Titus" (Romans 7:5–6).

". . . our flesh had no rest." We were really, really tired. Have you ever felt like that? Not sleepy-tired, but bone-tired, spirit-tired. The apostle Paul did. Not only that, he was surrounded by conflicts bearing down on him from all sides. And he was afraid. And depressed. (The apostle Paul—tired, afraid, and depressed?) What was God's response to his condition? *Comfort!* God provided comfort to Paul through the presence of a person.

What do people who have had no rest need? Easy answer, but often not the one people pick. They need *rest*. People who are depressed and afraid need *comfort*. Candidly, I know that there are many of you who have received anything but rest and comfort from those in your church. When you were tired you were given more to do. Or you were told to hide your fear and put a smile over your depression because it made God look bad. And when you tried to be honest, when you admitted your need, you were shamed into silence.

Listen: It is not God who takes issue with us when we are in a weak condition. He has sent us His indwelling Spirit to be the Comforter of our hearts. And He wants to send us "Tituses" to comfort us as well.

Keep your eye out for the Tituses. You will know them when

you see them. They will be the ones bringing comfort, even when it seems that you're so alienated from God and His people.

2. Rehabilitation

Rehabilitation is an interesting concept. It means "to restore something to its former state of excellence." To rehabilitate a house means to restore it to its original beauty and wholeness. With a little scraping, gluing, nailing, and polishing, a house can be made as good as new. If you pay attention during your resting time (instead of fighting it), you may discover all kinds of things that could benefit from a little rehabilitation on your part.

For instance, consider once again Paul's question to the Galatians: "Where then is that sense of blessing you once had?" The question implies that there was once a blessing that has now been lost. Their sense of blessing needed to be rehabilitated—that is, restored to its former state. The way Paul attempts to do this is to remind them of what they had evidently forgotten. As a result of their relationship with Christ they were sons, daughters, and heirs of God himself. They had been set free from the burden of pleasing God by measuring up to some unattainable standard. And all of this was because of God's actions, not theirs.

Sure, the Galatians were bombarded with opportunities to measure themselves spiritually acceptable on the basis of something other than Jesus. And sure enough, they looked away from the cross and began looking at themselves and each other. Paul did his part by reminding them of the truth that had brought them such joy in the first place (Chapters 1–4). It was now up to them— to remind themselves of the truth, to hang on to the freedom Christ died to give them, and to live lives consistent with their identity in Christ (Chapters 5–6).

If you're like me—and like many others who have been hurt by God's people—you have no doubt whipped yourself with the question, "What is wrong with me?" Or, "What is it about me that I always seem to find these unhealthy relationships and keep getting hurt like this?" In another context these can be self-blaming and unhelpful questions. But I suggest that you strip the attitude of self-punishment out of these questions and ask them with the attitude of an honest learner. Ask these questions for the purpose of taking responsibility for being better protected. Understanding yourself can keep you from repeating the scenario in the future. You are powerless to change anyone else, but you can change yourself. "What's wrong with me?" is a question others may use all too eagerly in a destructive way. But you can ask instead, "How can I be healthier and better equipped for future relationships?"

Maybe your answer is, "I don't have good boundaries." In other words, you can't say no, or you feel guilty when you do. Physical boundaries, like locks on doors, are the places where everyone else's space stops and your space starts. It is not disrespectful, selfish, or unspiritual to ask that others have permission to enter our physical house. Their job is to knock. Ours is to decide whether or not to let them in.

Yet many of us have been trained to believe it is wrong for us to have emotional or spiritual boundaries. It's unspiritual for us to think about what we want, or what is good for us and our situation. We never learned that it was sometimes acceptable to say "no." Or we have had it ingrained in us that if a need exists we are automatically supposed to do something to fix it.

And so we continue to allow other believers to barge into our relationship with God and others. And if we protest we feel selfish or "unsubmissive." Consequently, we don't protest at the time—but we most likely feel resentful later. *You can change this.* Taking responsibility for the fact that we act and think this way is the beginning. Doing what we need to do in order to get boundaries isn't the same as taking the blame for other people's insensitivity or intrusiveness. People are always responsible for their own intrusiveness.

A bit earlier we noticed that following the apostle Paul's journeys to the region of Galatia in Asia, there were some who came behind him, thinking it was their job to correct his teaching. In Galatians 1:6–9, he wrote that anyone who preaches a gospel contrary to the one he first delivered to them is to be "accursed"— literally, consigned to hell and destruction. Then Paul asks the rhetorical question, "Am I now striving to please men?" (v. 10). The implication is that if he were a people-pleaser he wouldn't have been able to write these harsh, difficult things. Paul was far more concerned with telling the truth as he had received it from God. He understood that he was accepted by God (See Romans 14:3, 4), while people's acceptance comes and goes.

Perhaps your period of rest has revealed that you do everything you can to live by these codes: "Nice is better than honest"; "Peace at all costs"; "It's my job to make sure no one else is unhappy." In fact, the reason you're deathly afraid of being honest is simply that you are afraid you won't be liked. So instead of telling people when you're hurt, angry, disappointed, or that you disagree, you smile and carry the weight of your feelings or opinions alone, and you pretend not to notice someone's inappropriate behavior when in fact you really do notice it. Eventually you avoid them, or gossip about them, or try to manipulate them to change. Or you may eventually ditch the relationship altogether.

Again, that person is totally responsible for his or her inappropriate behavior. But *you* are responsible for the pretending, gossiping, manipulating, or disappearing. You are as much responsible for a lack of true relationship with that person as they are. And once you realize this and take the responsibility to change, the relationship has a chance to be real—at least insofar as your efforts are concerned.

Changing the Things We Can

There is a famous saying by Francis of Assisi. Some know it as "the Serenity Prayer." It goes like this:

> Lord, grant me the serenity to accept the things I cannot change, the courage to change the things I can, and the wisdom to know the difference.

Unfortunately, lots of people do the Serenity Prayer backward. They spend incredible amounts of energy trying to change what isn't their job or what isn't even within their power to change. And they accept plenty of things that they could change if only they took responsibility.

One thing you and I can always change is ourselves.

Freedom and healing begins when we simply say, "Even if no one else changes, I can do things differently." You can learn healthy relationship skills. You can decide how to respond. You don't have to allow your life to be dictated by the agendas of others. Once you get your power to say "no" back (or get that power for the first time), you'll be able to discover the liberation and exhilaration of a heartfelt "yes."

It is not my goal to ramble on here detailing all the ways people can change to be more honest and healthy. Suffice it to say that life is a two-way street. We are responsible for what we contribute to it, and to our relationships—whether others contribute or not. If and when we decide to distance ourselves from a relationship— and that does become necessary at times—it is nevertheless our choice to leave, and we are responsible for it.

We are never "stuck" in painful circumstances because of other people. We can get unstuck making new choices. And with courage we can make those choices. Rehabilitation begins when we accept the power of choosing a new way to live.

There are four "R's" in your recovery, as I said. And now we'll look at the next healthy steps—releasing the hurt, and risking new relationships.

14

Letting Go and Moving On

As we saw in the last chapter, the apostle Paul was convinced that God was the provider of comfort for the weary. Largely, comfort came to him through Titus.

But, in fact, Titus gave to Paul "the comfort with which he was comforted in you" [the Corinthians]. And Paul says that God "comforts us in all our affliction so that we may be able to comfort those who are in any affliction with the comfort with which we ourselves are comforted by God" (2 Corinthians 1:4). The purpose of receiving comfort, of receiving any healing or restoration, is to propel us as healthier people back toward relationships. It's true that we cannot give away what we have not really received—but we never lose what we have been given in spirit by giving it away.

What keeps us from diving back into relationships? The next two R's of recovery address more roadblocks to healthy relationship-building.

Release

Earlier I said that with exercise I had been able to resume many activities my back problem had forced me to curtail. And there were also things I needed to do differently if I wanted to avoid future injury. For instance, I got a different bed. While it appears that this involved only one change, changing physical beds, there were really three changes that took place. First, I had to change my view of *what I needed* in terms of a bed. Then I *acquired* a new bed. Finally I had to *let go* of my old bed. In the absence of these changes I could have kept my old bed and suffered. Or I could have felt angry and resentful that I "had" to go through the expense to get a new one.

When it came to lifting I had to remember to lift with my knees, or else ask for help to lift or carry certain things. But first I had to accept a new view of myself in relationship to lifting. Then I had to lift differently. Finally I had to let go of the old view of myself as someone who was pretty much indestructible, because this whole incident was a stark reminder of just how fragile I really am. In the absence of these changes, I could have kept lifting in unhealthy ways, declined help, or even resented others when they offered help. Or I could have hated myself for needing help in the first place.

In these examples you can see that change brings gain, but it also brings loss. In the first case I gave up a bed. In the second, harder change, I not only gave up some lifting, I struggled with the thought that I didn't or shouldn't ever need help, or the belief that something was wrong with me if I did. Yet my back benefitted because I was able to let go of these beliefs and replace them with more realistic ones.

Acceptance—Letting Go of Control

Changing takes the wisdom to know what we can change. And then it takes the courage to act. In his prayer, Francis also asked God to give him the serenity to accept the things he could not change. It is both *helpful* and *healthy* to stop trying to control things over which we have no control. The restful alternative is to learn to let these things go. Some people seem to grasp this quickly. Others need time and help. But acceptance and letting go of things we can't change is our target.

Let me illustrate this principle by using scenarios reported to me by people who have been hurt in church:

I cannot control whether people heed my confrontations concerning their inappropriate behavior. I can control whether I choose to ignore the behavior, gossip to others about it, OR hold them accountable for it.

I cannot control whether people act in hurtful or helpful ways toward me. I can control whether I allow myself to continue in hurtful relationships by pretending not to be hurt, or whether I react in hurtful ways in return.

I cannot control whether people are happy with my efforts. I can control whether I make the effort.

I cannot control whether people continue to get themselves in messes. I can control whether I continue to bail them out.

I cannot control whether people respect or disregard my feelings, priorities, or gifts. I can control whether I say yes to other opportunities that make sense with my life and are consistent with the heart and abilities that God has given me.

I cannot control whether leaders in my church use money in ways that are wise and accountable. I can control whether I continue to support this particular ministry with my money.

I cannot control whether leaders use their authority to control, shame, and keep problems quiet. I can control whether I continue to submit to them or be part of that church.

I hope you can see that in addition to letting go of tasks on the outside, there are some rules and expectations for ourselves and others we can also let go on the inside. We must let go of the rule that says it's our job to please everyone, and the belief that we could if we tried. Unless we do, we are destined to find ourselves exhausted or hurt again.

Hurtful, irresponsible, and controlling people "need" to be surrounded with "fixers" and martyrs in order to stay hurtful, irresponsible, and controlling. If we don't want that job, we may need to change inside and out.

When we learn to let go we must be ready to encounter the very human experience of *grief*.

When my dad died I was overwhelmed with a sense of loss, mingled with intermittent periods of numbness. The thought *It can't be true* even crossed my mind when I was standing at his casket. Over the next year I went through the "if onlys." If only he . . . she . . . I . . . they . . . had done such-and-such. Then I moved on to anger. I blamed the doctors, myself, even my dad. Depression followed as the weight of my loss and my inability to change it sank in. Finally I accepted reality. "It's true. I'm sad. Things will never be the same. I will go on."

In the grief process we move from experiencing loss, to denying it, to feeling the crushing weight of that loss, to blame as we try to make sense of the "why," to anger as we rail against reality, to depression as the starkness of reality and our powerlessness to change things sinks in. Acceptance comes when we can let go of what we have lost, even while we still feel the pain, so that the loss no longer interrupts or controls our lives and relationships. From this place we can get on with what is next—trying again.

Risk

What have you lost? Important, even lifelong, relationships? Your investment of time, money, energy? Your innocence and integrity, because you tried and failed to play the religion game? Or maybe your idealism about what the body of Christ should be about? All of these things and more?

Was it a huge loss? Probably—so huge in fact that it took a while to sink in. Were there people who acted dishonestly, or unreliably, or in other ways they shouldn't have? There are many people to blame. Everyone is to blame—nobody is to blame—who knows who is to blame? And are you angry? Hurt? Sad? Disappointed? Perhaps all of these and depressed as well.

What's wrong with you? Nothing. You're normal. Our relationship with Christ doesn't turn us into unfeeling, unaffected spiritual zombies. If anything, it makes us more sensitive to what's real. The Holy Spirit didn't come to keep us free of problems, pain, and risk. He came to empower us to press through our struggles, and to comfort us when we get knocked around.

But there comes a time for acceptance—a time when we unhook from our losses, even while feeling the pain, and move on. Sure, after my surgery I no longer can hoist a canoe onto the top of a car. But I can still paddle a canoe. I have even found that I can help someone else when they hoist it. (You know what? I'm beginning to think that I should never have been hoisting it alone anyway.) Refusing to do the things we can do is a prescription for emotional, spiritual, and even physical stagnation. Refusing to pursue relationships with imperfect believers because we have been let down by other imperfect ones is the same prescription. We need to try again.

This prospect isn't without fear. This process isn't without risk. But it's the road we must take if we are to experience, not just know about, the provisions God has for us as members of His family. For all its fearfulness the risk is well worth it. The remainder of this chapter describes some of the risks we need to take as we get on in our relationships with others in God's family.

It's a Risk to . . .

. . . *have our own personal relationship with God.* The religions of the world place people in relationship with a system of beliefs or a set of rules. This isn't true of Christianity. While it might be hard to tell from looking around at Christians, Christianity, in its biblical essence, is about relationships between people: a person and God; a people and God; people with one another. While this is a book primarily about relationships among believers, a Christian's foremost relationship is with God.

The implications of this are vital.

First, we must never again live as if another believer is capable of meeting our needs, an especially important point to remember regarding religious personalities (leaders, speakers, authors, televangelists), because some will urge and even demand (even if subtly) that we place them in the place of God. And even when legitimately powerful leaders don't insist that we look to them, other people tend to. It is a very human thing to insert people we can see into the need-meeting role of the Person we cannot see. People are resources. They always fail when we treat them as our Source.

Second, do not ignore or tolerate dishonesty, manipulation, or twisted priorities of those who claim to have your spiritual best interests in mind. Question, confront, and even leave the relationship if necessary. Most people who let us down aren't evil, just imperfect. Enjoy rather than *depend upon* those uncertain people and what they have to offer. Allow people to be imperfect resources in their personal relationships and on their own journeys with God, and then depend only upon the certain One (see 1 Timothy 6:17).

Third, when imperfect people let you down, don't transfer your hurt and disillusionment to your Source. It's a risk to keep depending on the unseen Source when the visible resources are proving they're imperfect. It's the risk of faith. I'm asking you to take that risk.

God is our only Source. People and things are resources from our Source. We can only give away in our relationships with others what we actually have ourselves, and that is also true regarding what others have to give to us. Therefore, we must be tenacious in the ways we guard our personal relationship with our Source, and realistic in what we can expect from others.

. . . *have our own personal theology.* In 2 Timothy 3:14–17, Paul tells the young pastor,

> Continue in the things you have learned and become con-
> vinced of, knowing from whom you have learned them; and
> that from childhood you have known the sacred writings which
> are able to give you the wisdom that leads to salvation through
> faith which is in Christ Jesus. All Scripture is inspired by God
> and profitable for teaching, for reproof, for correction, for train-
> ing in righteousness; that the man [or woman] of God may be
> adequate, equipped for every good work.

My friend David Johnson is a lover of God's Word. He spends his life not only doing what the verses above encourage but chal-lenging and enlightening others through his preaching and teach-ing. One day he got a thank you letter from someone in his con-gregation who said that David did such a fine and thorough job of studying and explaining Scripture that the person felt he no longer had to study it for himself.

David was heartbroken. It's tempting for some believers to make others responsible for determining their theological beliefs. But believers need to interact with the Word of God themselves and formulate their own theology. I am not saying that we disre-gard the teaching, preaching, and theological viewpoints of oth-ers. I am saying again that these fellow believers of today and from the past are *resources.* You and I need to own our own personal theology.

If you want to get serious about this, go to your Christian book-store or library and acquire some good Bible commentaries. My criteria for a "good" commentary is one that (a) tells you what the writers of the Bible were saying, (b) what it meant to the original readers, and (c) ways in which it could apply to you today. The Holy Spirit and you will have to discover the ways in which the Word actually does apply to you today. You must then be empow-ered by the Holy Spirit in you to change.

. . . *set our own personal boundaries.* Not allowing the agendas or needs of others to dictate your level of activity will keep you from inserting yourself into the role of need-meeter. You are only one resource in a host of resources that God the faithful Source provides for others. Holy living and acts of service to others can't be coerced or legislated. Genuine holiness and acts of ministry flow out of love for God and others. As 2 Corinthians 5:14 says, "For the love of Christ controls us." Caring for others inside and outside of the body of Christ results from depending upon God to meet our needs, and giving away what He gives us.

. . . *forgive.* While forgiveness is an essential part of the process of moving on, for some believers it is an extraordinarily difficult task. When those who have wronged us refuse to take responsibility for what they have done or to acknowledge that their actions were wrong, forgiveness feels weak, like we're giving up control. We have lost so much, given so much, that the prospect of giving up even more seems like adding insult to injury. Forgiveness is risky, and we are *owed.*

In Matthew 18:15 Jesus presents a teaching on forgiveness that is most helpful and healing, once we understand its scope. He begins by telling us how to handle someone's sins against us in four basic steps. First, go reprove (confront) that person in private. If he listens (understands), the issue is settled. If he *doesn't listen* (understand and agree), go again and take one or two others to help keep the facts straight. If he *refuses to listen,* tell the church. The church, here, is not a group of people who meet in a building on Sunday. It is the group of people who have a genuine spiritual connection with you and the offending person. If he still refuses to listen, "Let him be to you as a Gentile and a tax-gatherer."

A Gentile was someone who wasn't in the same spiritual family as the Jewish people. He was an outsider, an outcast, like the Jews who collected taxes for the Romans. They were supposed to be on the side of God's chosen people but worked for the enemy. Notice here that Jesus doesn't say "make him be" as a Gentile or tax-gatherer, but "let him be." In other words, those who wound us and then won't take responsibility for the behavior aren't acting as family members. They're acting like outsiders, like people who are supposed to be on our side but who really work for the enemy. So let them be. Stay away from them. Staying away isn't the act that breaks relationship with them; it acknowledges the fact that they have already broken relationship and won't take responsibility for their actions so that restoration can take place.

It's interesting that Jesus follows this by a teaching on forgiveness (Matthew 18:21–35). Unfortunately for some believers, this is one of the most foreboding passages in Scripture concerning forgiveness—the parable about a servant who owed much, was forgiven much, and then refused to forgive even a little. It concludes with the ominous sounding promise, "And his lord, moved with anger, handed him over to the torturers until he should repay all that was owed him. So shall My heavenly Father also do to you, if each of you does not forgive his brother from your heart."

Yet there is good news and hope contained in this powerful story. You see, the king had offered forgiveness to a slave who owed the equivalent of $10 million. There was no way for the slave to come up with the cash, yet he responded to his dilemma by saying, "Have patience with me and I will repay you everything." This was a man who had no insight into the depth of his problem. He was not a broken person. And so while forgiveness was offered, it was not truly received. The "forgiveness transaction" that restores relationships didn't occur, and we know that because his heart remained hard.

In a little while this slave found another slave who owed him about $20. He demanded to be paid and his fellow-slave—who could eventually have repaid his debt—responded with the same answer the first slave had given to the king. "Give me some time." But the first slave showed no mercy and ordered him imprisoned, virtually guaranteeing that the debt could no longer be repaid.

Then real trouble comes to the unforgiving slave. The king found out what had happened. In essence, the gracious and bountiful forgiveness he had lavished on this slave was wasted! Disregarded. Treated with ignorant contempt. The slave who had received so much mercy had thrown it away and was pouring out angry brutality instead. And so the king ordered the first slave to get what he had deserved all along.

Now I have a few questions. Do you think the first slave would have had the second slave imprisoned if that "forgiveness transaction" had occurred? I don't. Rather, he would have been a broken person, and broken people are soft-hearted and compassionate to others who are broken. Was the first slave turned over to the torturers because he didn't forgive? No. His lack of forgiveness indicated that he was not broken. He hadn't received the forgiveness that was offered—and further, his relationship with the merciful king was still broken. How sad, when he could have experienced true, *from-the-heart* forgiveness.

Forgiving someone is like saying to them, "You no longer owe me anything. The debt is gone." How does this passage apply to your situation?

You could be the person who, because you're owed a lot for the hurts and disappointments you have suffered at the hands of other believers, chooses to make them pay for what they have done. That's a lot of work. First, you have to keep emotional and spiritual ledgers detailing what is owed. Second, the one needing forgiveness may never acknowledge any wrongdoing. It's possible to see the "torturers" as all the fruitless effort involved in *not* forgiving, and the pain-filled energy used to keep track.

Or you can rewrite the story. You can be the person who knows that you have been forgiven a debt you could never pay. And so you choose to release others who owe you a lesser debt. Most assuredly, it's easier to forgive someone who admits what they have done and repents. But it's possible even when they don't. And while it may not result in a restored relationship—because a "forgiveness transaction" hasn't taken place—*your work is finished and you can move on!*

If you struggle with forgiving those who have wronged you, stop trying. Don't spend a lot of energy mustering up enough *try-hard* forgiveness to reach your goal of "seventy times seven." That won't gain God's approval.

Instead, spend time turning your face toward God, basking in the reality of the forgiveness you have received for the debt you could never pay. Revel in the truth that you have been made a family member of the King of the Universe, an heir to all that is His. I am convinced that a day will come when you will pluck forgiveness like sweet, ripe fruit on a tree, and freely give it to the ones who have let you down. Then it will be real. And you will discover that one *from-the-heart* forgiveness is better than 490 *try-hard* forgivenesses. And you won't have to worry about the torturers after all.

. . . *trust.* "I can't trust you!" I hear these words from the wounded heart of a disappointed parent, a jilted friend, a husband or a wife crying out to their adulterous spouse. There's no doubt that our trust for others is eroded, even obliterated, when we've been hurt. But is it really accurate to say, "I can't trust?" I don't believe so.

I say this because trust isn't a feeling, it's a choice. It's the will to risk, invest, depend on, based on a belief that the other person isn't going to hurt you—that they're going to be trustworthy.

Consider this example. My daughter asks me if she may use the car. I ask her where she is going and when she'll be back. If she gives me an answer with which I can agree I give her the keys. In other words, I choose to trust her with the car. But let's say she returns home two hours later than she promised. The next day she asks me for the car again, and the whole routine replays itself—including the late return. When she comes to me the third day and asks for the car, it wouldn't be accurate for me to say, "I *can't* trust you with the car." Why? I could again choose to give her the keys. It's that I am choosing not to trust her. She has acted in ways that were untrustworthy, and I have decided not to invest. It's proven to be too risky.

Are there people whom you have *decided* not to trust? They have acted in ways that were unreliable, dishonest, even venomous. It would be most accurate to say, "I am choosing not to trust them." *I can't* means that you aren't able. It's victim language. *I don't* means that you are able, but you have the power to choose not to. And, in fact, your refusal to trust might be a wise choice! To invest, risk, or depend on them might result in more wounds and disappointments. You might well need to "let them be to you as Gentiles and tax-gatherers"—people supposedly on your side, but who work counter to your well-being.

There's a danger here. You could choose to never trust again someone who just *once* shows they aren't trustworthy. But that isn't as dangerous as the next step: deciding not to trust anyone. That would be an incredibly unwise choice. "I won't trust!" are the words of someone destined to remain wounded, isolated, and lonely. Rather than "I can't" or "I won't," it would be better to say, "Right now the prospect of trusting again terrifies me, so I don't." This leaves the door open for God's healing, and for you to make different choices at a future time when you're better prepared.

Getting Our Trust Right

While Scripture tells us to love one another, exhort one another, comfort one another, be kind to one another, nowhere does it command us to trust one another! Yet trust is an integral part of any growing relationship. The cover of Pat Springle's very wonderful book *Trusting* says that trusting is "the issue at the heart of every relationship."[1] I couldn't agree more. It's not possible to have relationships with people without investing in them, without risking the possibility that they may let us down.

We will never enter into the wonderful, supportive fellowship

[1] Vine Books, a division of Servant Publications, Ann Arbor, Michigan, 1994.

of "one anothers" unless there is first an element of trust. Comforting one another can't take place in a relationship where there is shame for even needing comfort in the first place. Yet in deciding not to trust, ever or anyone, we actually victimize ourselves again by depriving ourselves of the resources God provides to help us live healthy, meaningful lives.

Where, then, do we get strength to choose to risk again? One place is relationships with trustworthy people. As we're loved, comforted, encouraged, and treated kindly by others, we grow in our belief that trusting them is a wise choice. So we choose to trust more. This results in further loving, comforting, and kindness, which again results in more trust. And while this places a heavy burden on Christian relationships, it is not an unwarranted expectation of the body of Christ. After all, God himself designed relationships with others as resources for His sons and daughters. These relationships are important, the risk involved great. No wonder He gives careful instructions concerning how to act toward one another.

There is another infinitely more powerful relationship from which we can gather strength to once again move toward relationships with God's people. David says, "It is better to take refuge in the Lord than to trust in man. It is better to take refuge in the Lord than to trust in princes" (Psalm 118:8). First and foremost we must depend upon God.

The phrase "take refuge" is from a Hebrew word that means "to trust," yet it's a different word than the one used in reference to trusting man and princes. It has the connotation of *trusting with reckless abandon.* If you had to choose whether to trust God with abandoned recklessness or to trust human beings, though in a far more conservative and measured way, choose to recklessly trust God. Why? Because God is our Source, and people only resources.

Paul illustrates this principle in 1 Timothy 6:17: "Instruct those who are rich in this present world not to be conceited or to fix their hope on the uncertainty of riches, but on God, who richly supplies us with all things to enjoy." The problem with riches isn't that they're evil. It's that they're uncertain. So rather than *fixing your hope* on the uncertain thing—the resource—fix your hope on God and *enjoy* the resources. Our relationships with God's people are also resources, and being so they are also uncertain. So fix your hope on your certain Source and enjoy the uncertain resources, precisely because the resources *are* uncertain, and the certain Source never changes.

When we put our hope in God, we can allow uncertain things to be uncertain without being destroyed. We grow free from our demand that others be unfailing. We gain enough internal freedom to accept what they may offer. Because we understand that what they owe us pales in comparison to what we have, we grow in the power to forgive as well.

The next chapter is about moving toward relationships with God's people once again. It's about finding a church where you can trust and be trusted, give and receive. Crazy? I hope by now you don't think so. But I am including a list of criteria I think will provide you direction in finding a healthy church—when you are ready to try again.

15

When You're Ready to Try Again

Over a decade ago a friend and colleague of mine was involved with a Christian ministry in the Twin Cities. He had been in a leadership position with considerable responsibility within the organization for a number of years. After a split with the founder of the organization, he left and continued his ministry under a different umbrella. It was painful for everyone involved, resulting in hard feelings for the way numerous issues were handled. And there were plenty of perspectives on the reasons behind the schism. Of course, who was right and who was wrong depended on who you talked to. One of the explanations was that the two leaders' personalities simply were incompatible.

Recently I had a conversation with my friend and he told me he had arranged a meeting with his former supervisor. These are men who had worked closely together for five years, then dodged each other for the next ten. My friend called the meeting because he felt it was time for them to resolve their differences. While it was clear to my friend that they would never work together, he hoped to work to a point where they no longer totally avoided each other. Perhaps they could even converse when they found themselves at the same functions. After all, both of them are Christians.

"How did it go?" I asked.

"Do you know what he said?" my friend replied with a disconcerted tone in his voice. "He told me that because of our personalities we probably would never be able to have any kind of fellowship together."

189

When I heard this I remembered a recent experience from a trip to the Christian Booksellers Convention in Denver. One afternoon Holly and I rode the bus from the convention center to our hotel with two Christian men. One was a black social activist, the other a former high-ranking member of the Ku Klux Klan. Once bitter enemies, they had now written a book together about the power of God to obliterate every barrier that separates people, about His amazing ability to heal and restore relationships.

Neither Type-A nor Type-B

In the working world it's true that some people can't work together. Taste, style, habits, and personalities mean everyone won't be best friends with everyone else. But unable to fellowship as believers because of personalities?

If there is any place on this planet where people can fellowship together *despite* their personalities, it's within the body of Christ.

Earlier we saw that Paul, in Ephesians 3, wrote about the "mystery" of Christ, explaining that the existence of the church signaled to the rulers in heavenly places God's renewal of humankind. He tells exactly what that evidence is:

> . . . as it has now been revealed to His holy apostles and prophets in the Spirit; to be specific, that the Gentiles are fellow heirs and fellow members of the body, and fellow partakers of the promise in Christ Jesus through the gospel (vv. 5–6).

In Colossians, Paul tells us further that we are ". . . being renewed to a true knowledge according to the image of the One who created [us]—a renewal in which there is no distinction between Greek and Jew, circumcised and uncircumcised, barbarian, Scythian, slave and freeman, but Christ is all, and in all (Colossians 3:10–11; also Galatians 3:27–29).

Jews and Greeks, slaves and freemen, barbarians and Scythians? God's power spanned a great chasm between opposing groups of people who had never gotten along—who had literally been at each other's throats. But as a twentieth-century, midwestern American, it's hard for me to grasp the breadth of that chasm and the utter miracle of that new God-forged bridge. Still, I believe the kind of fellowship experienced by the two men on the bus in Denver—which can only be attributed to the power of God—is the new unity Paul is talking about. To "update" Paul's teaching, I could say that God is so powerful that in Christ He could span the chasm between a converted Jew and a former Neo-Nazi. With the renewing work of Christ, Bill Clinton and Rush Limbaugh could fellowship together!

What about men and women with different personalities? Yes, God could even bring them together. He just needs people with new hearts, dependent upon Him, who are willing to love one another as Christ loved them—that is, with humility and with the heart of servants.

What about you?

Another Chance

Earlier I told the story of Baby Joe. When he was born he had no idea what was in store for him in his physical family. And he had nothing to say about the behaviors, character traits, or priorities of that family. None of us can choose what our family will be like. It's an impossibility.

But what if it wasn't impossible, and we did have a choice? What if, prior to actually becoming part of a family, we were given guidelines to help us look for a healthy family? We could use a resource like that to find a healthy family whose priorities we agreed with, in whom we could find love and acceptance, and through whom we could learn and practice loving others.

We do have this opportunity when it comes to our church family. We do have a choice, and guidelines do exist. The New Testament tells us some of the things we can expect in our spiritual family, among them support from another, love, a place to be in process.

Based on those guidelines, here would be some questions I would ask:

- Do people in this family care about things that really matter?
- Do they respond to people's mistakes with grace and patience?
- Are the people in this family gentle and giving?
- Or are they mean, caring only about themselves?
- Is telling the truth more important than image-management?
- Does honesty get sacrificed in the service of maintaining false peace?
- After being with this family for a while, do I have a growing

dependence on the work of Jesus—do I revel more and more in His love?

* Or do I feel emotionally and spiritually heavier as time goes on, and less qualified to be a family member?

Baby Joe got a second chance. Somebody found him. Someone rescued him and introduced him to people who were committed to nurturing and equipping him to live a meaningful life. You have another chance as well. I hope that in these chapters you have discovered that you aren't crazy for feeling let down. I hope that you have gained permission to be in a healing process. And I hope you have glimpsed of what is yours as a son or daughter of a God who loves you and is patient with that process. I now want to give you some practical criteria that will aid you in your search for a church in which and through which you can become a functioning member of the body of Christ.

Avoiding Hurtful Churches

In *The Subtle Power of Spiritual Abuse*, David Johnson and I identified common characteristics of spiritually abusive systems. When these traits are present they make the relationships in that spiritual family hurtful. I would like to use those characteristics of grace-less churches as a starting point from which to venture into our discussion of the characteristics of grace-full churches.

In hurtful churches you find the following seven characteristics:[2]

1. *Power-posturing*. Those in leadership positions spend a lot of time and energy reminding others of their authority. Authority is used to boss and control members of God's family.

2. *Performance preoccupation*. How people act is more important than what's really going on in their lives. *People* aren't what is loved and accepted. *Behavior* is the most important thing.

3. *Unspoken rules*. How relationships function is governed by rules that aren't said out loud but, in many cases, have more weight than the out-loud rules or even Scripture. The most powerful and damaging of all the unspoken rules is the "can't-talk" rule. This rule keeps the truth quiet because the problem itself isn't treated as the

---

[2]For complete discussions of the related characteristics of hurtful and grace-full families see *Tired of Trying to Measure Up* and *Families Where Grace Is in Place*, published by Bethany House Publishers.

problem—talking about it is treated as the problem. People who notice problems and confront them are labeled divisive and disloyal. People shut up and call it "unity."

    4. *Lack of balance.* There are disproportionate focuses and values placed on certain areas of the Christian life. For instance, you must agree that certain gifts of the Spirit aren't for today or you're labeled "unstable" or "deceived." In other churches, if you *lack* certain spiritual gifts or don't exercise the gifts in ways accepted by the group you are considered a second-class Christian.

    5. *Spiritual paranoia.* There is a sense that people, resources, and relationships outside the system are unsafe.

    6. *Misplaced loyalty.* A sense of loyalty is built to programs, things, and people, rather than to Jesus.

    7. *Secretive.* Certain information is deemed suitable only for those within the church or only for certain people within the church.

Finding a Grace-full Church

    It's unlikely that one church would exhibit all seven of the characteristics I just mentioned. Conversely, it's likely that even in a healthy church you could find one of these traits, or some inkling of these dynamics from time to time. But wherever even one of these dynamics is present in God's family, people are apt to get hurt. And without exception, churches with a "can't-talk" rule will be extremely hurtful to their members. In these places problems can't be confronted or resolved because you become "the problem" for talking about the problem. Consequently, the offenders are isolated from accountability and the ones hurt isolated from healing. There is no chance for the healing that true unity in Christ brings.

    The characteristics of grace-full, healthy churches are opposite of those described above. The degree to which the following characteristics are found in a church is the degree to which members of God's family can grow in honest, healthy relationships with one another and God. These dynamics best characterize grace-full churches:

    1. *Authority and power are used to serve, equip, and empower.* In Matthew 23, Jesus says that the greater leader is the one who is the servant. This is the distinguishing mark of leaders in the Kingdom of God. Likewise, in Ephesians 5, Paul describes the "head"

as the person who treats the life of another as more important than his own. The kingdom of God is the only place where you find these definitions. It's as if Jesus and Paul are handing us a dictionary to help us understand what things mean in the kingdom. You can find bloodthirsty CEO's in corporate America. In legalistic religious families you can find tyrannical heads and leaders. In emerging nations you can find despot leaders who call the shots and punish anyone who disagrees. But not so in the kingdom. People who use their authority to these ends in the kingdom have no authority, at least not from God.

Spiritual authority isn't taken or asserted. It doesn't come because you hold a titled position, receive a degree, or get a salary. It is given by God for the purpose of shepherding God's flock. In grace-full churches, those with authority use it to serve, build, and liberate the members of God's family to be successful in the Lord's call on their lives. They do not use it to manipulate or control.

Respect for authority isn't demanded by getting puffed up or loud, or by using God's Word as a sledgehammer. A person who has to spend a lot of time reminding people of his or her authority—and as much energy demanding that people yield—does so because they have no real authority. True authority is *noticed*. In Matthew 7, the gospel writer says of the Lord that when He had finished teaching, the crowd was amazed at what He had said. Why? "He was teaching them as one having authority, and not as their scribes"—that is, those who had the title and who demanded respect for their position, but had no authority.

What a rebuke this is to many Christian leaders. I received a letter from some parents in Florida whose children were sexually abused by a man in their church. The pastors (who were also leaders in their church-operated Christian school) used their position to quiet and even drive away anyone who tried to hold this man accountable and to get the children help. After all, if someone needs help for being abused, someone must be doing the abusing. These leaders were only concerned with protecting their image in the community. They were worried that people would leave and that giving would drop. Besides, the perpetrator was related to a teacher in their school. They weren't willing to risk losing the teacher. Even worse, they demanded respect from these hurting parents for their actions, and used religious rhetoric and Bible verses to pressure and shame them for wanting outside help!

Rather than *demanding* our respect for their authority, those with true authority—who use it for the reasons why God gave it—*command* our respect with their faith, integrity, and consistency. In 1 Peter 5:2–3 Peter tells leaders to ". . . shepherd the flock of God among you, exercising oversight not under compulsion, but voluntarily, according to the will of God; and not for sordid gain, but with eagerness; nor yet as lording it over those allotted [literally, the inheritance—that's you!] to your charge, but proving to be examples to the flock."

2. *Believers are fighting the "good fight of faith."* Ask yourself whether you're being encouraged to depend more on Jesus to walk more fully in your spiritual inheritance. Or is the message just, "Try harder this coming week to be a good Christian," or, "Do such-and-such in order to live up to the spiritual standard"? These questions represent my own little test. I have frequent opportunities to visit various churches as I travel, and seldom do I go away from the morning service or Sunday school class or Wednesday evening fellowship without knowing where a church stands on these matters.

Embrace teaching when it encourages you to embrace Jesus. Then you will be around believers participating in the same struggle you are—the fight of faith. Try-hard messages indicate that people fight to live by their own religious self-effort—will worship—and call it "God" if they measure up to the list. This kind of church is a religious version of the world's systems, which also withhold love and acceptance until our behavior measures up. Yes, you may be welcomed with open arms as a *visitor*—but as a *member* your walk with God will most likely be wide-open for the scrutiny and criticism of all who "know" what your spirituality should look like.

Not one of us is above accountability. But frankly, our relationship with Jesus is too precious to allow it to be dragged through the mud. In 1 Corinthians 4:3–4 Paul says,

> But to me it is a very small thing that I should be examined by you, or by any human court; in fact, I do not even examine myself. For I am conscious of nothing against myself, yet I am not by this acquitted; but the one who examines me is the Lord.

We should listen to the exhortations or confrontations of others when they encourage us to spiritual freedom in Christ. But the only approval we need to be concerned about is God's—and we have that because of Jesus. In fact, even in those cases when those who scrutinize our performance are wrong, it is *still* Jesus' actions toward us that validate us, not our personal innocence.

At this point, I must issue a disclaimer: I'm not saying that obedience isn't important. It is. I'm not saying that right behaviors don't matter. They do. But our "works" must be as a result of faith. Holy living flows out of hearts dependent upon God.

In Colossians 2:6 Paul says, "As you therefore have received Christ Jesus the Lord, so walk in Him." You didn't come to God with a list of your accomplishments in order to earn His approval. You came by faith, depending upon His power to move you from death into life. Live your life dependent on that same power to conform you to the image of His Son.

In Philippians 3:17 Paul says, "Brethren, join in following my example, and observe those who walk according to the pattern you have in us." What example, what pattern is he talking about? Actually there are several found right in this chapter. Here are some of them:

Verse 1: *Rejoice in the Lord*, rather than looking to your religious behavior as your source of joy.

Verse 2: *Watch out for those who would point you toward religious behavior* instead of Jesus.

Verse 3: *Glory in Christ Jesus and put no confidence in the flesh.* That is religious self-effort.

Verse 8: *Count as loss everything you used to lean on, for the sake of knowing Christ.* In Paul's case this was the best list of religious behaviors anyone had ever seen.

Verse 9: *Be found in Christ having a righteousness through faith*, instead of trying to derive righteousness through performing lawful Christian behaviors.

Verses 12–15: *As those who are right now perfect and complete* (in Christ. See also Colossians 2:10), *forget what lies behind* (Paul is again talking about his religious behaviors) *and lay hold of Jesus more and more, so that He may continue to make you even more perfect.*

Verse 16: *Keep living by the standard you have already attained* by being in relationship with the only true Standard-attainer.

In Philippians verses 17 and 18, Paul issues strong warnings to believers to watch out for those who would hold up religious behavior as the means to righteousness. In fact, he calls "enemies of the cross" those who add anything to the cross of Christ as a means to God's acceptance. Why? Because they perpetuate the idea that the cross isn't enough. Beware of them and the churches they attend.

3. *Rules are spoken about out loud, and they are biblical.* In a grace-full church, God's rules are important. But God's rules are to serve the ones He loves and to help their lives and relationships work better. He didn't give the rules as a means of earning His approval. He gave His Son so that we may receive His acceptance, and that as a gift.

Consider these two scenarios. Just after you cross the Highway 70 bridge from Minnesota into Wisconsin, there is a sign that reads: BUCKLE YOUR SEAT BELTS—IT'S OUR LAW! In other words, do it or else! But this can be said in a different way. Because I wasn't raised in a seat belt-conscious era, I oftentimes forget to buckle my seat belt. But my daughter Erin is acutely aware of the wisdom in doing that, thanks to driver's education and the media. Every time she gets in the car with me she buckles her own seat belt, then looks over at me and says, "Papa, buckle your seat belt." Both Erin and the State of Wisconsin are right, because I could die if my seat belt wasn't buckled at the time of an accident. But Erin's exhortation comes in the context of a relationship. She loves me and has my best interest in mind, so she prescribes a behavior. That's why God gave His rules, and that's the spirit in which we should approach them.

When a rule is broken, it is the behavior healthy people reject, not the person. Romans 8:1 says, "There is therefore now no condemnation for those who are in Christ Jesus." While God might hate some of our behaviors, He still accepts us. The rest of Romans 8 is testimony to the fact that nothing and no one can separate us from His love. The Holy Spirit *convicts* us of our behavior. Legalism *condemns* the believer and calls God's acceptance into question.

Even in the case of church discipline (1 Corinthians 5), there are two goals in removing a person from the fellowship. The first is to protect the sheep from someone who is unrepentant and having a negative influence on the flock. The second is to benefit the person and even attempt to bring him back into Christ and into fellowship (see 2 Corinthians 2).

Not only are God's rules there to benefit us and our relationships, they are based on Scripture and apply equally to everyone. Don't confuse traditions or people's obsessive/compulsive religious habits with scriptural precepts. And if a rule favors a certain person (the spouse of a leader, for example, or people who have been there the longest, or the loudest people in the church business meeting), or if a rule is too silly or rigid to say out loud, it shouldn't be a rule. It is wrong to hold people accountable for rules they didn't know were operating, especially rules that are too goofy to write down and pass around.

4. *Deference to the True Head of the Church, His agenda, and His methods.* People are wounded in churches where more authority or wisdom is ascribed to people just because they have an education or to people who "don't need one," because they get all of their teaching right from the Holy Spirit. Or because they exercise certain gifts of the Spirit—or don't, because they are dispensationally "enlightened." Or because they are related to a religious celebrity through whom God is doing mighty works—while others are treated as spiritual third cousins, once-removed.

In grace-full churches, gifts of the Spirit are appreciated as *gifts.* Even religious training is looked at as a gift. And people are gifts to the church from God, placed there just as He sees fit. Everyone needs everyone else and greater honor is intentionally directed toward those whose actions or positions don't naturally draw honor in their direction (1 Corinthians 12).

Grace-full churches belong to God, not people. People are simply stewards, table waiters, of the resources God provides, and not owners. I once attended a conference where the speaker posed this question: "Can the True Head of the church do anything He wants to at your church?" It hit me like a ton of bricks. Because at that time the answer was "no." Jesus couldn't change the agenda for the missions budget. He couldn't have a different opinion than the group of people who started the church. He couldn't show up in any ways that we couldn't control or explain. He couldn't even change the order of service if He wanted to.

Just because we do things in God's name doesn't mean God is doing it, or even in it. To write "Church" on the door or stationery sometimes results in a case of mistaken identity. If we insist on our church being *our* church, we risk hearing Jesus say, "Behold, your house is being left to you desolate!" (Matthew 23:38). Literally, "I leave to you the house of *you.*" If Jesus has left your church, is that a place you really want to be?

5. *Our safety is in Christ, and so diversity is welcomed.* "Greater is He that is in you than he that is in the world." Even as an immature, mostly inappropriate, and unregenerate adolescent I used to think, "If we're as right as we think we are, how come we're hid-

ing in this church building? Why is it necessary to avoid everyone?"

In 1 Corinthians 5:9–11, Paul speaks with clarity to the matter of thinking that our safety is in staying away from people outside of our group. Because our safety is in Christ, who lives on the inside, we don't have to avoid those on the outside—which, as Paul reminds us, isn't possible anyway. In Hebrews 13:5–6, we are reminded that Jesus himself has said, "I will never desert you, nor will I ever forsake you," so that we can confidently say, "The Lord is my helper, I will not be afraid. What shall man do to me?"

An outgrowth of finding our safety in Christ within us is that we can welcome and associate with a diverse group of believers. I recently spoke with a woman who moved with her husband back into the area where his family lived. They began attending the family's church and initially felt welcome. As time went on, however, they were taught that this church was the only true church. Since their baptism was the only one that counted, this couple would need to be rebaptized in order to be accepted into full fellowship. Also, visitors and nonmembers weren't allowed to take communion. They could watch from the balcony.

If a church's so-called safety is in doctrines, traditions, and stepping inside church walls, then you will always be asked to divide from other members of God's family, and for a variety of reasons. Some churches divide you from others based on whether a day in Genesis was a 24-hour day; whether Jesus is coming back before, during, or after the tribulation; the length of people's hair; whether hymns or choruses are sung; or issues of "religious politics" too numerous to mention.

If the personal relationship with Christ that made you a member of His body doesn't qualify you for acceptance in a local manifestation of that body, or if you have to go through another "spiritual rinse-cycle" in order to be accepted, what would make you want to stay in such a system?

6. *Loyalty to Christ and the building of His kingdom takes precedence.* "You shall love the Lord your God with all your heart, and with all your soul, and with all your mind. No one can serve two masters."

These two statements that Jesus made are pertinent here. Pastors, programs, denominations, doctrine—these are all resources from the Source, given to serve us so that we in turn can serve others. While it may be appropriate to affiliate, gravitate, commiserate, congregate, or cooperate, it is never okay to elevate, capitulate, or be found prostrate before anyone but *the Lord.*

One of the outgrowths of tenacious loyalty to Jesus is unity with other believers. People are brought together when they depend upon their common Source, and they become involved in the common cause of building His kingdom.

7. *Presence of honesty and openness.* In safe, grace-full churches, honesty matters. Being able to notice and talk about reality matters more than how things look. Finding the truth is more important than being right. Secrets cannot survive in an environment of truth and honesty. In fact, they aren't necessary.

There is a difference between issues that are private and confidential and those that are a secret. There are things that aren't the business of the entire church, such as how you or another person struggles with a certain problem.

While your income isn't any business of the pastor, his or her salary is your business. And the way you conduct that business is through competent, wise, faithful people to whom the financial affairs have been delegated. Neither are the salaries of the church staff a secret—but in my opinion, they should be kept private. There are certainly many church matters that should be kept confidential, and not made matters of public discussion. But watch out if what is private is also kept secret from those who legitimately hold responsibility.

In Closing

As we conclude, I would like to share one more tool you can add to your relationship toolbox. I believe it will be helpful to you as you embark upon or continue in your search for a healthy church. Let me cite again from Pat Springle's excellent book *Trusting*, in which he helps us learn who and how to trust again:

"It is foolish to:

- Trust people who consistently wound you.
- Believe people who consistently give double messages.
- Think intimidating people have your best interests in mind.
- See people as all good or all bad.
- Withdraw from all people because some have hurt you.
- Try to figure things out by yourself.
- Seek advice from foolish people.
- Avoid conflict at all costs.
- Stir up conflict.

- Be too self-disclosing in order to earn others' love or pity.
  "It is wise to:
- Call on God and wise people for help.
- Be cautious about trusting people.
- Slowly elevate your level of trust in others as they prove their trustworthiness.
- Be honest with most people about your feelings and desires.
- Withhold your feelings and desires from abusive people.
- Be realistic about the growth process of learning to trust perceptively.
- Forgive and love, but not necessarily trust, others.
- Expect conflict when you are honest.
- Learn to communicate clearly and calmly with all kinds of people who mistrust.
- Realize that even trustworthy people will sometimes fail you."

The writer of Hebrews tells us that it's important to ". . . forsake not the assembling of ourselves together." This is not about the ritual of going to a certain geographical location with a certain group of people at certain times during the week. This is about relationships that build God's people and spread His kingdom. My goal in this chapter has been to present some things to remember when looking for a safe church, one that is building the right kingdom.

When the actions and attitudes of God's family members toward one another breach the "family contract" found in the New Testament, people experience the "fine print" of the Christian life. Believers feel hurt, disappointment, disillusionment, and fear trying again. Outside the church, the world that so desperately needs to find life in Jesus thinks the church is irrelevant.

When we live consistently with who we are and what we have as His people, those of us in God's family experience what He has promised us. The world then might even respond to the working of Jesus' body the way people responded to the work of Jesus: "They were all amazed and were glorifying God, saying, 'We have never seen anything like this'" (Mark 2:12).

Please try again. Though you have suffered and lost, there is a lot to gain—for you, for the lost around you, and for the whole family of God.

One Final Word

In the first two chapters I talked about the "wolf," Satan, the fact that he is out to destroy the body of Christ, and that he will use whatever means he can to do it. As the apostle Paul says in Ephesians 6:12, "For our struggle is not against flesh and blood, but against the rulers, against the powers, against the world forces of this darkness, against the spiritual forces of wickedness in the heavenly places." I have spent a lot of time in this book talking about the very real wounds we receive in church relationships, those flesh-and-blood places in our lives. I have given some guidelines to help you find flesh-and-blood places that will be safer and more healthy. But as Paul says, we are in a spiritual war. So I would like to revisit that theme as I close.

In Matthew 4:9, amid the spiritual war going on between the devil and Jesus, Satan offers Jesus a substitute. He shows Jesus all of the kingdoms of the world and says, "All these things will I give You, if You fall down and worship me." Was the world really so much under Satan's influence that he could offer it as a reward for Jesus' loyalty? I think so. Notice that Jesus doesn't say, "Ha, Satan, these are not yours to offer." Instead, He answers, "You shall worship the Lord your God, and serve Him only." You know the rest of the story. Because Jesus always clung to the Father, even through crucifixion, the kingdoms of the world will all be His anyway.

The wolf is still in the business of offering substitutes—the kingdoms of the world in exchange for the kingdom of God. What does it look like? Appeasement instead of peace. Uniformity instead of unity. Toleration in place of appreciation. Patronization rather than honor. Tickling ears over "speaking the truth, each one with his neighbor, for we are members of one another." Control, programs, and expedience supplant spiritual authority, people, and process. And when we settle for substitutes, people get hurt. I'm not talking only about hurt feelings. I'm talking about *hurt*, the bite of the wolf. And the greatest casualty of these . . . is love.

You have felt that bite. Somewhere along the line the "spirit of the wolf" crept into your church, or perhaps had hid there all along, waiting to take advantage of handshakes, smiles, and fellowship that turned out to be plastic. And you are bleeding from its bite. What should you do now?

Don't give up! Notice what Jesus did. He kept His focus on His heavenly Father. You can do that too. Paul precedes the Ephesians passage above by saying, "Finally, be strong in the Lord, and in the strength of His might. Put on the full armor of God, that you may be able to stand firm against the schemes of the devil." In other words, hang on to God. I'm not saying, "If you just trust God your troubles will magically disappear." I'm saying, "Keep going toward your Father."

And don't just *have* faith. Take up a *shield* of faith. The Roman shield, to which Paul refers, was as tall as the person carrying it, soaked in a fire retardant, with hooks on the sides so that warriors could actually attach themselves to each other and build a wall. Sometimes they would hunker down behind the wall to withstand an attack. But when they decided to advance, the wall of warriors was a more formidable force than many individuals attacking alone.

The same is true of the church. We are safer together than we are alone. And we are also more dangerous to the enemy. If you are too wounded or tired right now, rest. But at some point there is one more thing I want you to think about seriously. If you look at the parts of your body protected by the various components of God's armor—loins, chest, feet, and head—you see that you are protected from attack from every side except one: your back. You still need someone to cover your back. That someone is the body of Christ.

So try again—for your own sake, for the sake of other believers, and for the sake of His mission—delivering people out of darkness into the kingdom of light.

For information on seminars or tapes
on this and other church- or family-related topics contact:

DAMASCUS, INC.
P.O. Box 22432
Minneapolis, MN 55422
(612) 537–0217